HOME RANGE

Essays on the Land

Annette Chaudet

Cover Design: Antelope Design

Photography by the author.
Pronghorn Antelope Photographs Pages 126 & 130
by John Belobraidic—johnbphoto.net

www.pronghornpress.org

Dedicated to everyone
who loves the land as I do,
and to those who seek to understand.

Contents

HOME RANGE

Essays on the Land

Presence of Place

I remember the first time I came across Gretel Ehrlich's book, *The Solace of Open Spaces.* I was jealous. That title—those five words—encompassed exactly what I feel about living in this part of the West. I was sorry that I hadn't thought of it myself because the truth is that I am greatly comforted by this endless landscape that surrounds me.

My relationship with the West has always been—and still is—with the land itself, the look and the smell of it, with the huge sky and with the absence of other human inhabitants. But much to my surprise, I find a great number of the people who live here in the West are more interested in the history of this place, than in the place itself.

Unlike me, they see the land in terms of its history in relation to the people who have passed over it or lived on it. I find this curious. Intellectually I understand it, but it doesn't fit into the way I relate to the place where I live. For me the connection is based on a visual perception tied directly to my soul. And so I find their fascination with the past completely foreign to my own context.

When I ask friends and acquaintances why this interest in what seems to me an overly romantic version of this country's historic past, they look at me blankly. They don't understand why I don't share their enthusiasm for endless stories of hardship and suffering, of life and death as it once moved and is, in fact, still moving, across these vast open spaces.

I recently read a book, recommended by no less than three friends, about hardscrabble ranch life in Montana. It left me cold and I began to wonder if maybe this longing for history is some sort of genetic carry-over from those European ancestors who made new lives, here, in this new world. I admit that the theory I've developed is only writer's flight of fancy, but I often imagine complicated scenarios to explain the things I don't understand. It may be only a device, but it is entertaining and allows me to define and comprehend the otherwise unexplainable. It goes something like this:

Much of the Rocky Mountain West was settled late when compared with other parts of the country. Many immigrants came straight from old country to new. They found land that looked a lot like what they'd left behind though, no doubt, much grander in scale. Scots came to a craggy land where they could graze sheep. Many of the Scandinavians found themselves in the dense forests of the upper Great Lakes. Germans, comfortable with snow and mountains, settled in the sometimes green valleys along the front range of the Rockies in Colorado, Wyoming and Montana. But let us remember that often those who came directly from Europe to the West, found life here no more difficult than what they had left behind and, despite setbacks, one of more opportunity and freedom.

The immigrants seemed more than willing to adopt their new country and throw themselves, full swing, into the taming of virgin land, but I wonder if, somehow, the need for knowledge of the history of this new place was passed down to their children and grandchildren.

For the settlers, there *was* no history of their new home save a scrap or two of knowledge gleaned from those who had arrived not all that much before them. Certainly, few bothered to learn anything from the natives, who, for the most part, had either chosen to or been forced to move on. But think of the history these Europeans left behind—several thousand years of conquering and being conquered and, before that, the doings of the ancient Gods who toyed with the fate of mankind under their care. From the people who survived came reasons for, and stories of, the aspects of the landscape, itself.

Surely, both the written and the oral history in the old homelands gave a sense of permanence and purpose to the lives of those people, no matter how difficult. When they finally arrived in this new world after the hardship of the passage, the newcomers were cast adrift in a land so big that they never had to worry about bumping up against the end of it. But it was a land with no recognizable reference points and, from their perspective, not much in the way of history. Could it be that this displacement caused some sort of longing for history in their descendants?

A major part of what I dislike about the recounting of the history of the West is the lack of emotions involved in the telling. We read tale after tale of who went where and what happened. But the narrators never mention how their subjects felt. Granted, it's hard to impose emotions on someone long gone, and I might accuse the fans of this sort of writing of imagining what the people felt. This is also why I dislike non-fiction and prefer fiction where the writer is free to imagine the characters' emotions and motivations. This, for me, in historical context, is much more memorable, enjoyable and informative. It allows me the luxury of imagining how I might have felt in similar situations.

Take, if you will, one example of what I consider unfounded projection of emotions which has become an accepted interpretation and one which I find particularly irritating: the mystique of the strong, silent cowboy. He doesn't ever say much. Some people insist it's because he has so much to say that he doesn't know where to begin and so doesn't speak at all. I ask them to consider that he says nothing because he has nothing to say. Whether this comes from lack of introspection, absence of philosophical thoughts, or from simplemindedness remains to be known. But I think it should be considered.

And so, have we come full circle? I don't share and hence don't understand the fascination of those who live here with the history of the area. What I've read seems to be a romanticized version of the past. Yes, it was hot and there was no air conditioning a hundred years ago. But the early settlers didn't come from an air conditioned environment. Hot was still hot here in their new home, cold was still cold. Water was closer or farther away, sweeter or more alkaline, but the plumbing was still the outdoor variety. Then, as now, anyone involved in raising either crops or animals, no matter where they are, will always find themselves and what they produce at the mercy of the weather. Wisconsin and Arizona are no exception. Neither is Florida nor Maine. Fishermen suffer today from bad weather and poor catches, as they have for thousands of years. Better equipment can help ease the work load and the dangers but convenience leads to larger undertakings in all these endeavors and to greater losses when fortune or weather takes a turn for the worse.

I am interested in history, but my interests lean toward stories of how someone adapted to their surroundings. I want to know the emotions involved in the transition. In historical pieces, I want the first-hand version, the letters or diaries. In modern accounts, I prefer to hear from someone who comes from the "big city" and decided to "rough it" in some out of the way place. It is easier for me to relate to solving that sort of problem, to identify with the hazards and solutions of adapting to the unfamiliar.

I remember reading a book, at least twenty years ago, called *The Snow People* by Marie Herbert. It was the story of an English woman who followed her anthropologist husband to a point on the arctic circle where he had gone to study the Inuit. She had never done this sort of thing before and she had a baby with her who was less than a year old. It was a brave undertaking and one not at all necessary. She could have stayed home. For me, the story—her story—of adapting to unimaginably unfamiliar and sometimes dangerous situations was fascinating (as well as humorous). I'm sure I would have been less interested in her husband's conclusions about the history and daily lives of those native people.

I was born in Virginia. I remember the woods behind my school and the colors of the leaves in the fall. But we lived in the city and I had no opportunity in those early years to spend time in a rural setting. I was too young to have learned to love the land in that part of the country by the time my parents, both California natives, moved us back to the sunshine state when I was seven.

Though I've spent the last forty plus years along the front range of the Rockies, there's something to be said for growing up with a beach not too far away. Certainly, in a huge city which is mostly concrete, the sea is one of the few ways to get close to nature without driving for hours into the mountains in an attempt to rise above the smog.

History of place in a big city tends to be what is forced on you by your elementary school teachers. It was always hard for me to imagine Yangna Indians and their wickiups when I looked out on an acre of paved parking lot. Even the Spaniards were hard for me to picture in such a cityscape, unless I made a pilgrimage to San Juan Capistrano and could experience the momentary isolation of place within those mission walls.

Those of us who live in cities develop our own relationship with the urban wilderness. We have familiar trails we take to certain places. We learn what's safe and what's not, how to avoid the perils in our environment. We learn where to go for the things we need and how to go about finding new sources for necessities as well as pleasures. But when I lived in the city, I longed for nature. The manicured lawns and flower gardens were not restorative. When I lived in Los Angeles, only the sea or the mountains could resurrect my spirit. And the sea was much closer.

When I was sixteen, my family made a visit to Boulder, Colorado. We drove out from California. I was too young at that time to admire the often barren landscapes of Nevada and Utah. Perhaps the appreciation of subtleties comcs as we grow older. Then, wilderness, for me, had to be green. When we drove into Boulder, slapped up against the rocky facade of the Flatirons, I was convinced it was a synchronistic event tied, somehow, to the sight of Maria spinning around in joy on that grassy hillside at the beginning of *The Sound of Music*, which I had seen the previous fall. I'd told myself then, that such was the landscape in which I wanted to live. I never once considered that I could only find it in Austria, and sure enough, Boulder supplied an adequate approximation.

Three years later, I moved there. In the beginning,

I spent all my free time exploring the dirt roads that laced the mountains, winding in and out of old mining towns and around isolated cabins, some still occupied, others in various stages of melting back into the meadows. Every turn in the road presented a new picture–perfect vista, and I, like most newcomers, was overwhelmed by the sky. In my last nine months in L.A., I had caught sight of the mountains that surrounded the basin only once. You can imagine the comfort I found in a sky that was vast and blue and clear. The smell of fresh air and the land itself can be a revelation to someone who has grown up in a large city.

Those first two years in Colorado also taught me a few lessons on the subject of things-are-not-always-as-they-appear. I remember making several determined tries to picnic in grassy, flower filled meadows, only to discover that they were, in fact, bogs. I slowly realized that in the West, any place lush and green means a lot of water that comes from a lot of snow. The lushest spots spend the winter and a good portion of spring in deep snow that only liquifies during the summer and, quite unromantically, provides an ideal breeding ground for an unpleasant variety of biting insects.

Six years after leaving L.A., I found myself in Wyoming. I was swept away by the unlimited horizons and skies that were even bigger than Colorado's. The unbelievable abundance of wildlife and complete lack of people enchanted me and was the first harbinger of my latent hermit tendencies. I struggled for four years with low wages and impossibly chauvinistic attitudes toward working women. Finally, after one winter that hit sixty-five below zero *not* counting the wind chill factor, I gave up and went south to Denver where at least I had some hope of earning a decent living.

There I was, in a fairly big city again, still longing for the wide open spaces. The then-clear view of the mountains wasn't enough. A friend soon lured me to Santa

Fe for a visit and in New Mexico I found the sky again, along with a town that seemed consumed by the pursuit of the arts. To me it was the perfect combination and I spent eighteen years there, some of them very difficult, but always in a landscape that I loved. Even in that oldest of North American cities, I had no interest in the history. It didn't matter. All I had to do was see the land—to *smell* it— to understand. And there *is* a smell there, an essence of sun-warmed, sandy soil, piñon pine and just a hint of sage-brush. It's delicious.

Much to my surprise, I ended up leaving New Mexico and returning to Wyoming where it still seemed possible to find affordable housing in a small town where people were friendly and crime, by comparison, non-existent. I also found a land that I wanted to embrace, literally. Only the abundance of low growing cactus prevented me from falling down on the ground, spread-eagled to absorb the wonder of it.

I finally settled in a tourist town with busy summers and quiet winters. It seemed ideal, and proximity to Yellowstone National Park was a very important factor in my decision.

I've always loved the Park and kept the memories of its landscape close, even while I've lived in other places. Also, I've always considered Yellowstone *mine*. Personally. I'm content to let others manage it and deal with it on a day-to-day basis. It can be visited by millions, and enjoyed by all. But it is mine. And when I need something a little more varied and startling than the wide Big Horn Basin to set my eyes on, I can lose myself in the Park.

I guess it comes down to the fact that place for me is purely visual. Maybe it's the artist in me, but I am enraptured by the scope of the land itself. This is something I see, and through the seeing, feel. While I can find some sort of beauty almost anywhere, it is the ability to look out over miles of this country and see nothing else. And most important; it comforts me. Both the absence of "civilization" and the hugeness of the space makes me feel both safe and secure.

Lately, I've been moved to descriptions of the land that brings me so much solace. I try hard to observe, to describe exactly how I see, in an effort to share my impressionistic observations as a painter might share a painting. I want to give someone else a chance to look through my eyes and feel what I feel, if only for a moment. Perhaps that is what we, as writers and artists, are always striving for—the language of art. And because no two people see anything exactly the same way, perhaps we also seek validation of our vision. At any rate, these efforts fulfill a need in me to understand why it is that I am so connected to this land.

Earth, Sky and Time

Looking out across Badger Basin, it is impossible to place the scene in a precise cubbyhole of time. If you can see a dark spiderweb of pipe which signals the machinations of the energy industry, then you can narrow it down considerably. But if, from where you stand, you see nothing to indicate the presence or passage of humans, your window to both the past and the future is considerably larger. If you are not constrained by a deep knowledge of geology to remind you just when this particular piece of terrain was covered by an inland sea, then it's quite easy to believe that you are looking many thousand years into the past or, surely, a very long way into the future.

This view has a quality of timelessness simply by virtue of size and the absence of human interference. Definition in this kind of land comes from nature, not from man. Here, in the part of the West that slams up against the formidable barrier of the Rockies, your sense of the land is, by necessity, defined by the sky. Here, when you look out across the contours of the earth, you accept that the land is only half of what you see.

This equitable division of the view sometimes offers a stark separation by color but, more often, the palette is subtle. Yet it shifts constantly, governed by light and temperature, moisture and wind. Bright spring green land touches shades of storm cloud grey, summer green and gold nudge pale blue, autumn yellow vibrates against deepest turquoise. Even winter, which can bring a monochromatic white on white and make the view all one, can surprise you with a quilt of green and gold, rust and purple patched over white and spread against a blue you thought long gone.

It is all part of earth and sky working together, with or without you there to see and take sustenance from their effort. It is simply there, simply the way of things as they have been in the past and will be in the future—land and landscape touching the sky, beyond the boundaries of time.

Rain Clouds

A rainy day in Wyoming is a treat for me. While I doubt I'd be happy in a place where it was the norm, here, along the front range of the Rockies, skies are sunny year round and moisture most often welcome. We've had a very dry spring this year. No late snow blanketed the ground at Easter and there was no rain until about three weeks ago. Suddenly, it seemed like spring with some sort of showers almost every day. Then it was fall again for a week and there was snow halfway down the foothills as the thermometer plummeted to thirty degrees. For the last week it has been warmer with either showers or drizzle every day.

This morning I'm not displeased by the grey sky as I head toward Billings. Most times I'm grateful for the one hundred and twenty mile commute to civilization. A two hour drive through a varying landscape is soothing in a way that being stuck in traffic on a freeway for the same amount of time most certainly is not. In all these miles there is only one stop sign going my direction.

At the highest point passing Heart Mountain, the fog of moisture in the air silhouettes the rows of foothills and flattens them so that they look like the painted cardboard layers of a stage set. This fog has erased the peaks completely and the world has shrunk down to a cozier size.

Despite my personal preference for unlimited vistas, there is a comfort to being enclosed by the curve of the land and a low, grey sky. The clouds hang so low they look like a cottony layer of packing material, covering the earth, protecting it. Landmarks are king size in the West. We navigate by mountain peaks rather than green freeway signs. When the weather shortens our view it is a little disorienting.

Spring is finally tangible, a concept you can wrap your eyes around. The moisture in the air intensifies the greens and makes the whole world seem clean. It washes away the nearly invisible coating of dust spread so evenly by the relentless wind. If the rain continues throughout the day, perhaps the more serious accumulation of mud will vanish from my car...if I can avoid the dirt roads until they dry out.

The grass is thick and lush. The weeds in the borrow pit look knee to thigh high. It's amazing what a little moisture can do for our land that is usually so dry. All this green will feed the deer and elk as well as the rabbits and mice that, in turn, make meals for the coyotes and hawks. There is a sense of well being and renewal here, a feeling that all is as it should be.

Coming up onto the bench, the peaks are still invisible but the landscape is broad enough to give the advantage of watching the weather move over the wide plateau. It's Mother Nature at work in cinemascope and

I never tire of it. The clouds are many shades of grey from a soft pearl to a heavy laden ash. Each has a form of its own, distinguished from the next one by its color.

The river is milky-muddy today, cappuccino color as it curves back and forth beneath the highway, changing course each time it is crossed. This could throw off your sense of direction were it not for the fact that the road hits an occasional high spot that allows you to glimpse the whole snaky layout. No matter which way it runs, it is relentless and determined to get wherever it's going. In the places where the river spreads itself shallower over a greater width, it manages to add a little green to the color mix, but the overall brown says it has been raining for awhile.

Crossing the line into Montana brings a drop in altitude and more farmland. Sage gives way to the order of man's imagined mastery of the earth. The alfalfa looks thick and healthy though the other day a farmer told me that it really needed some sun. The barley looks so full and perfect that I have the urge to run through it like some carefree woman in an allergy medication commercial. Not very practical, especially in this weather.

Some of the sandstone cliffs that pop up here and there along the highway are so thoroughly dampened by mist and windblown rain that they have darkened to shades of taupe and clay. This doesn't happen when the rain is more direct and falls straight down, but this type of precipitation changes everything. Even the weedy lawns look thick and pristine in this weather.

A tractor stands alone in the middle of a field, stopped mid-plow. Disking mud is a tough business. There is one field where it looks as though some hay has been mowed along the fence but it lays there on the ground, unbaled. The wind picks up and I spot a single red wing blackbird, hunched, bobbing back and forth as he clings to a wildly waving cattail. The leaves of the poplars turn their silver sides to the wind and change their appearance completely.

In this weather you don't see very much wildlife. Even the cattle seem to thin in the fields. I suspect they have the shelter of a cliff or wash somewhere, staked out for just such an occasion. But I do see a soggy pheasant picking up seeds along the edge of the pavement. He doesn't seem to be bothered by the wet.

A train has derailed here—recently—where the tracks parallel the highway. There are a few cars scattered between road and rails, some are upright, others on their sides. There is also a pile of huge wheels which must attach to the shipping containers like an old-fashioned pair of roller skates and make boxcars of them so they can go from ship to rail and continue on their way to the marketplace. I think more often of seeing those containers on flatbed rail cars. But there are none here, only containers and wheels. Is this new? New to me, certainly.

Several men in bright orange ponchos are prowling the tracks near what remains of the wreck. Have they found the cause or are they checking the repairs?

I pass a skunk casualty but the moisture has contained his signature super-chlorophyll aroma. The wet fur looks sad. Was he running for cover when he was struck down?

By the time I finally get on the interstate for the last sixteen miles that will take me into the city, the sky opens. The clouds mover higher, piling up white above the rimrocks. They seem puffed up with pride at delivering all this water. Beyond them, there is a hint of blue.

Annette Chaudet

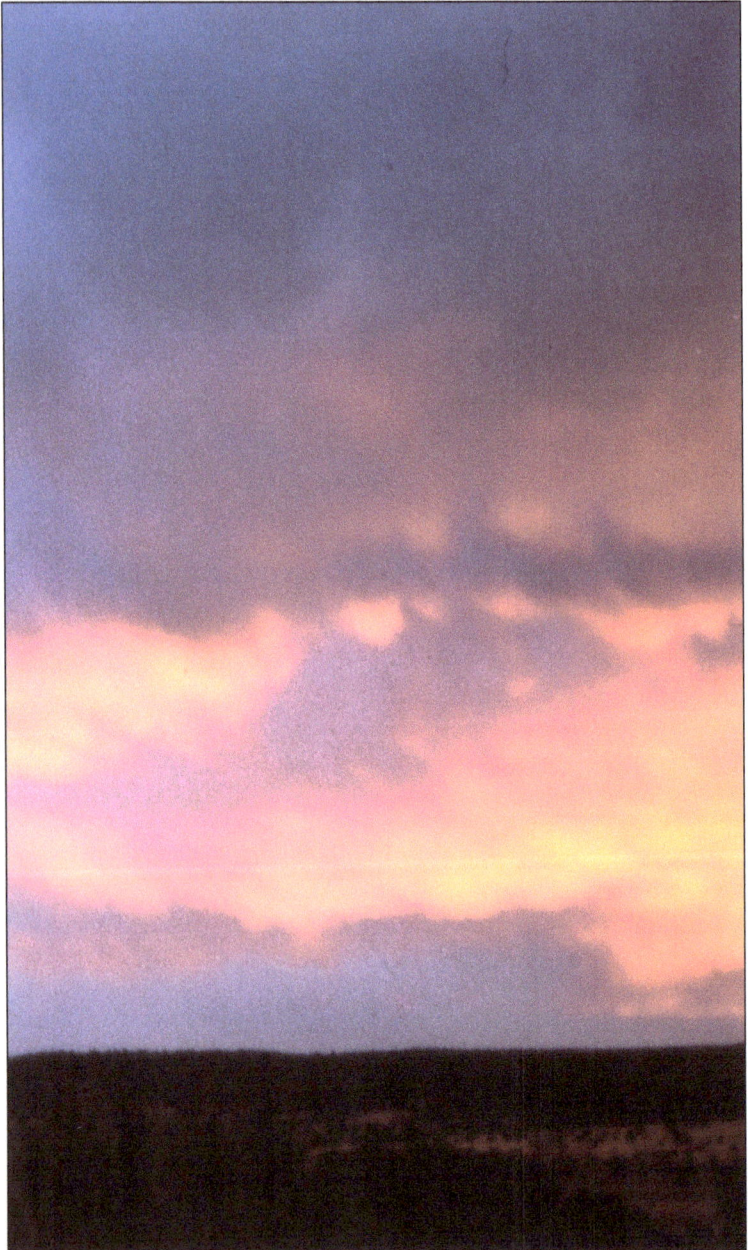

Skyblue Pink

I don't often have the opportunity to drive south from Cody. Adventures in that direction usually either mean a trip to Casper, which is about four hours, or on to Colorado. So tonight I am happy to make a quick run to Meeteetse.

I've always liked Meeteetse, a tiny town with an odd name. Strangely enough, the doctor I had growing up in L.A. was born there! It truly *is* a small world.

I've always considered Meeteetse an interesting little pocket of green between Cody and Thermopolis. I had friends there for many years but they have since moved to Cody and so my reasons for going that way are few and far between.

We've been suffering from a heat wave these last twelve days. Usually our summers are marked by three or four days where we close in on one hundred degrees. This extreme heat often causes a build up of the clouds along the front range and the blessing of a quick afternoon shower to take the edge off. Instead of that pattern, this year has been too long with no relief in the form of even a sprinkle, so I was expecting to view the varying terrain to the south through undulating waves of heat. But, as usual, Mother Nature is unfailingly unpredictable and at about three o'clock this morning the breeze came up and the temperature dropped a good twenty degrees. It almost makes me giddy.

The drive down Highway 120 is consequently full of surprises, not the least of which is the overall sense of green. It's a full summer-bloom chartreuse in the late afternoon light. I say "afternoon" but it's 8:00 p.m. Measuring with my outstretched arm, I place three fingers between the sun and the horizon. At fifteen minutes per finger I calculate the sun disappearing just before nine. We may not be in the land of the midnight sun, but these northern latitudes certainly give us light late into the evening this time of year.

I'm only making a quick delivery and minutes later I've turned north again. The breeze has been with us all day and grows a little more vigorous as the sun drops. The beautiful yellow sweetclover bobs and bows in the space between the asphalt of the highway and the pale wooden fenceposts on either side. There are shorter grasses growing at the bottom of the borrow pit that wind through the bigger plants like a pale, straw-colored stream.

The shadows lengthen and darken the soft contours of the hills. They always look to me like a huge fawn colored cloak carelessly discarded on the surface of the earth, remaining where it fell, the fabric bunched and wrinkled. The hills on the east side of the road have lost their gentle curves and have worn away leaving rows of uneven badlands pyramids, streaked with ivory and plum.

On the dark side of the undulating ground, the sagebrush remains a cool blue-green, almost as if dimly lit from within while its branches are a dark taupe. It is truly my favorite color combination, one I seek to reproduce in my yard. It's not the same though, when surrounded with the green-green of a lawn. Still, my Russian olives at home mimic the many grey-green shades of sage and provide a hint of Mediterranean colored comfort.

In the distance I can still see a little snow on the peaks, but it's patchy now, a spot here and there. The clouds are starting to build up behind the mountains to the southwest. The wind has caught them and spread them out like a handful of flour flung into the air. While admiring this formation I can hear meadowlarks, singing their grand finale to the day.

I pass a small catch basin, dozed by a rancher to hold water for the grazing herds. It reflects a dull, rather than shiny, silver. But what is it reflecting? The sky above remains blue. Perhaps it is only the presence of the light itself bumping up against the more solid element of water.

The sun drops low enough to be in my eyes and suddenly my car is being tailed by its own long shadow, big enough at first glance to seem another car entirely. As I follow the curve of the highway it reorients itself to my left, almost as though it were determined to pass.

The dandelion puffballs are backlit by the lowering light and look like bubbles hovering along the side of the road. Brown and black cattle graze on the high ground between the shadowed ravines, a perfect abstract study in beige and sage, flecked with sienna and black. Here and there the leaves of a few scattered young cottonwoods glow in the lambent light. I can also pick out a small group of antelope. The only thing giving them away is the white of their rumps against the monochrome landscape.

There is endless visual variety in this land through the work of the seasons, of color and of light. I long to settle myself into it, high enough to look out across it day and night, to become a part of it and it of me in the most visceral sense. I want all that is here to grow through me and twine with my body as well as with my soul. It is an ache and a need within me and I can't say why except that my love for it is all encompassing.

The sun drops dramatically into the clouds above the mountain and suddenly a huge beam of golden light explodes through a break in the formation like a strobe through the keyhole in a sci-fi movie. The sun sinks farther and the beam dims.

To the east, the hills go pink and purple as the ball of the sun sinks farther below the horizon. The sky above them is softer shades of pink and lavender. But to the west, the sun sends its rays through more breaks in the clouds and fans them out in a perfect half circle above the silhouette of the ridgeline. What a light show! Heart Mountain, straight ahead, purples but remains darker than the undulating rows of the front range behind it, each ridgeline fading to a softer shade than the one before it.

When the sun is finally gone, the little clouds above the mountain turn an impossible shade of pink against the blue sky. If you saw this depicted accurately on canvas, you would swear the artist had gotten it all wrong, but here it is. The tossed flour clouds to the south have taken on the look and color of country fair pink cotton candy. What a wild palette!

Is it just too corny, this infatuation I have with these visible manifestations of the natural world?

I truly believe there is a good reason make sure that all children have some chance to experience rural landscape. Those raised in the shadowy canyons of the inner city must have an opportunity to see the land, to see those creatures that live on it in freedom, to touch the animals that provide them with sustenance. How else can they come to understand how wide their world truly is,

how vast the possibilities? How else can they come to
know their part in it? The scope of the land itself makes
violence unnecessary, undesirable. The bigness of it
encourages cooperation. It gives us a proper perspective of
our own place in the grand scheme of things.

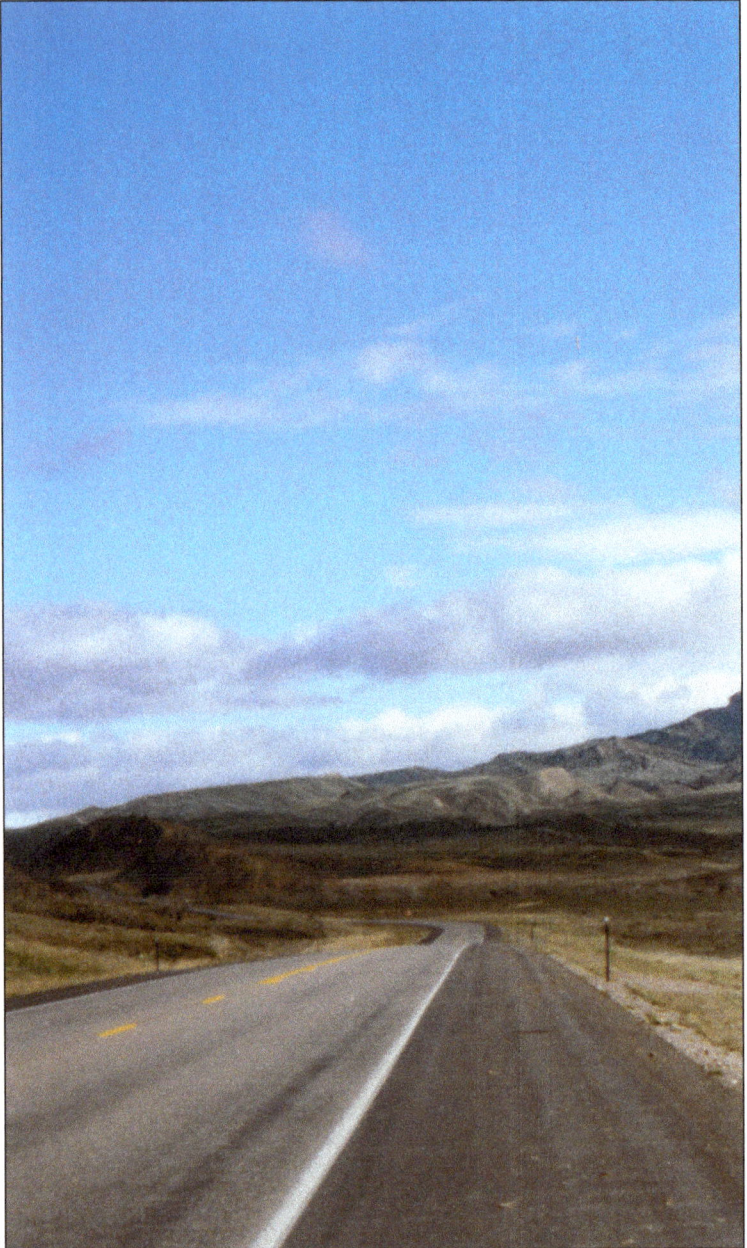

Going South

I didn't get out of town til 7:00 a.m. this morning, two hours after my scheduled departure. I have a genetic disability, one I suspect I've inherited from my mother, that makes me stay up almost the whole night before a trip, trying to get ready to go. It's insane but I can't seem to stop doing it, no matter how I plan. In addition, if I have a long drive ahead of me, I prefer to leave at 4:00 a.m., (this, a habit inherited from my father) so that by noon I will have traveled a good distance and will be able to call it quits before dark. Having gone to bed at 3:00 a.m., one hour of sleep was out of the question. Three has proved to be not much better.

Nonetheless, I'm excited to be going and am fairly alert. The light at this hour makes the land yellow. The blue green sage is almost grey against the yellow grasses. Two ravens in a row sit atop the fenceposts, like a couple of cranky sentinels, drying their wings in the morning sun. I spot a few antelope out in the sage. It's rained the last few days and, still lying down, they seem to be enjoying the warmth of early morning sunlight.

The tall slender grasses, seed heads heavy, take on the color of old ivory as the light comes from behind while the sculpted hills are streaked with shadows from the low angle of the sun. In places the rocks stack up, each one smaller as they rise like some strange, mystical cairns left by a race of giants long since departed.

The powerlines south of Meeteetse are held up by pylons which, to my surprise, are made of wood. The V shaped brace in the center combines with the horizontal and vertical supports to give them the appearance of angry baby owlets flapping unformed wings in anger at the staring intruder. They seem to be the only unnatural thing on the land in the long, mercifully empty stretch between Meeteetse and Thermopolis, except for a few large tanks marking the oily resources below.

Some of the dried grasses have taken on a pale pumpkin color as though they anticipate the fall, which is beginning to hint at its impending arrival in the coolness of the rainy nights. But that season seems far away when the daytime temperatures still hover in the nineties.

There are a lot of patches along this road that have been seriously over-grazed. Eroded and damaged, not a badlands sort of situation but rather one that has supported too many cattle for too long. I wonder if this is leased land— if the Bureau of Land Management should be doing a better job. Take away the leases? Fine the rancher? Surely something can be done to save this ground that I, as one of the citizens of this country, own. It will take many, many years for this fragile environment to right itself.

Flying down the two lane strip of asphalt I see the

marker balls that float on the high voltage lines and am reminded of a recurring dream that involves an inflatable airplane. I don't have it often, but it returns periodically, much to my delight. In the dream I carry this peculiar plane to the airport in a normal size and not too heavy suitcase. I walk to the edge of the runway, open the suitcase, remove the plane and blow it up like a child's water toy.

It's that strange transparent pinky orange plastic, the color of mercurochrome. When I blow it up it's proportionately the size to me that a pedal car is to a child. I can nearly touch the ends of the wings with my outstretched hands. It looks like a cartoon plane, round and stubby with an inflated propeller on the nose. I taxi down the runway and fly off up a narrow canyon. I always fly under the powerlines, but it is no feat of daring, rather that the plane is small and I can do it easily. Usually, about this time, I'm having so much fun that I laugh and wake myself up.

Time becomes liquid for me on these cross country trips and I think that may have something to do with why I enjoy them so much. As I enter Thermopolis, I can see clouds piling up to the south. I hope it means some rain but not enough to slow me down. I'm already behind schedule. I love the views heading south from Thermop toward Wind River Canyon, gently sloping slabs of land that end suddenly in a steep drop. Buffalo jump country.

At the entrance to the amazing canyon the water of the river is a perfect sky blue. In the spring it runs as red as the hills above it where the new grass screams in vibrating contrast. The canyon is beautiful at all times of the year, though very different at different seasons. This morning the sun is just clearing the top of the cliffs, so there is only a narrow line of light falling on the stone on the western side, leaving the rest in shadow. This stretch of highway can be treacherous in the winter when it remains patchy with ice everywhere the sun's warmth fails to reach.

The geology here is impressive and for people like me who have no background in that science, the formations are boldly labeled. Jurassic, Triassic, Cambrian. The dates are here, too. This would be something to learn, though I have little faith in the ages that science gives to the earth and her inhabitants. I'm sure it is far older.

Where the sun tops the rim and directly illuminates the water it turns the same color as the sage, flowing like liquid serpentine. I always thought this might be a canyon I'd enjoy floating. Wild rides through the rapids don't interest me and this seems suited to my lack of courage.

The rocks in some parts of the canyon are black. Is it lichen or a smokey reminder of the fire that made bare, branchless sentinels of the trees in one section? Despite the blackened remnants, there's quite a variety of vegetation here. I see a sign at one of the few driveways withing the canyon's confine that says they have apricots. I can't believe they have a crop, though the sun warmed stone may protect them from the harsher winter temperature drops.

At the south end the canyon opens up on Boysen Reservoir, a strangely barren landscape despite all that water. I've always fancied this lake as a perfect spot for a scene in a sci-fi movie. Beyond the lake, flat land turns gently terraced in the distance as I approach Shoshoni.

I'm always surprised to see a sign indicating the presence of a Masonic Lodge in a town as small as Shoshoni which lists its population of 635, a number which must include a large part of the outlying ranches. It's hard to imagine there are enough Masons here to even make up the officers. And yet all over the small towns of the West you see the signs for the Masons and the Eastern Star. I was one of Job's Daughters myself, and I wonder why the girls of Job's Daughters, the Rainbow Girls and the DeMolay boys don't get signs, too. It would certainly make these little towns look more lively and inhabited.

I remember one year and a snowy drive back from Denver. The road from Shoshoni to Casper can be a dull 102 miles in good weather, but harrowing in the winter. It took me five and a half hours with chains to cover that distance and there were a number of cars off the road. I felt quite fortunate to have made it through.

On this long straight stretch my mind reaches out to encompass the landscape, its few variations combined with the scope. Just as we have to be taught to see art in order to appreciate it, we must be taught to see and appreciate the landscape around us. It must evolve with our consciousness as we grow.

When we are young, we should start small, see the colorful spider in the garden, the blades of grass, and move up the scale of life until we pass beyond the food chain and into the environment. As I've said, it bothers me to think that this experience is denied to so many city dwellers. Truly, it should be required that children, through school programs, be able to spend time in a rural setting. Even growing up in L.A. I spent a weekend at a camp near Lake Arrowhead that was a school experience. It had a lasting effect. Obviously.

La Mer de Ciel

Sometimes, hours on the road, a snippet of long unused French flashes through my consciousness. I took French in high school but it was nearly twenty years before I was able to visit France. Needless to say, half forgotten exercises were useless. While living in Santa Fe, I signed up for French at the community college and was fortunate to find myself with a wonderful teacher. I took classes for five years and made lasting friendships with some of the students as we continued our only half-hearted attempts to study the language. Nonetheless, I had an easier time of it on my next trip abroad.

I find that long unused vocabulary comes back to me, albeit in bits and pieces, at the most unexpected moments. And so it is today as I drive north from Medicine Bow and into the Big Shirley Basin. *La Mer de Ciel* (the Sea of Heaven) is what pops into my mind as I study the sky. It is bright blue, as big as ever and supporting a flotilla of puffy, flat bottomed clouds, all drifting west. I watch them, a cinemascopic presentation that, if I were to stop the car and stand beside it, would become the even bigger IMAX version. Even after so many years, this land, and its other half, the sky, stun me.

It is this experience of the immensity of the land which I think everyone, at one time or another, should have a chance to experience. As Garrison Keillor once pretended, perhaps we should institute a Wyoming Space Administration. Afterall, it is something we have more of than most, no rocket fuel required. I admit that as residents of a relatively empty state, we are not all that interested in having a couple of hundred million visitors descend on us just to feel the scope of our land. So I'm willing to allow this idea to move into the realm of entertainment. IMAX would be a perfect format.

Here's my show: All fifty states. OK, maybe an hour won't do it but two surely will. For continuity sake, we should start in the East, Plymouth Rock, perhaps. Aerial shots zooming in on the rocky coast, lighthouses, crashing waves. Follow the edge of the continent south to the tip of Florida and the keys before turning north again. You would have to zig zag north to south and back north again, up and down to cover all the variations of terrain.

We would see the natural wonders from whatever perspective emphasizes their beauty. The biggest demand an overhead view, a daring helicopter shot of Niagara Falls, skimming the Great Lakes, treetop shots in the Minnesota wilderness that show why it is the Land of Ten Thousand Lakes. But then move over the land, through the woods at eye level. Catch the salt marshes of the Carolina coasts at sunrise for an exact rendering of what Pat Conroy writes about so eloquently. Find out what people love about their land and commit it to film. We're not interested in the friendliness of the people or the amenities of a particular area. This show is about the *land*.

For the vast territory of the West, Hawaii and Alaska, much could be seen from above, quickly skimming Maui and Monument Valley, Denali, Devil's Tower, Mount Rushmore, the Grand Canyon. Yellowstone will require a little more time and IMAX has already captured this beautifully, but it belongs in my show, too!

The camera stands on the ground next to a Saguaro and pans up so you can feel its size and strangeness. I'm sure that what is common to some areas could be as strange as sci-fi to people who have never seen it before. Don't we all need to really know the land that makes up our country? Wouldn't it serve as a poignant reminder of how precious our natural environment is?

It seems so many people never have the opportunity to appreciate the wealth of what our small portion of the planet offers. For all its troubles, there is so much to be loved in this world. Sometimes, I think we've forgotten.

Such are the musings of a creative if not too disciplined mind. An hour has passed and those ship shaped clouds seem to have caught a southern current and now float directly overhead, low to the ground at this altitude and patching the rolling surface of the earth with shadows the grey-purple color of old lady crepe. The sagebrush here grows in the wrinkles of the drainage and the indented tracks of thousands of covered wagons. The basin is all over green.

I spot what I think may be antelope but are in fact only bare spots on the ground. Then, within a half mile I come on a group of five of those amazing creatures right next to the fence. My expectation may have manifested them! Of course it could also be because this area is home to the largest herd of pronghorn in North America. I remember driving this highway years ago and seeing a dozen bodies at a time by the side of the road, no doubt wiped up by a single fast-moving semi. There were no speed limits in Wyoming then. I'm grateful that today the body count from my windshield survey is zero.

This is my very favorite spot on the drive between Colorado and Wyoming. While others prefer the speed of I-25, I stick to the back roads and more interesting views. If I could live anywhere along this route, it would be here, between Medicine Bow and Casper on a highway that often succumbs to winter and southern Wyoming wind. The number of snow fences alone might give one pause but the views are spectacular. It feels as though you can see all the way to South Dakota and Nebraska from up here with nothing to impede the view.

Apparently, residency is not an option. There is no sign of any habitation. This is oil country and, I assume, public land. If I were to find it was privately owned, I would indenture myself to the owner for the rest of my life, just for the privilege of planting myself here.

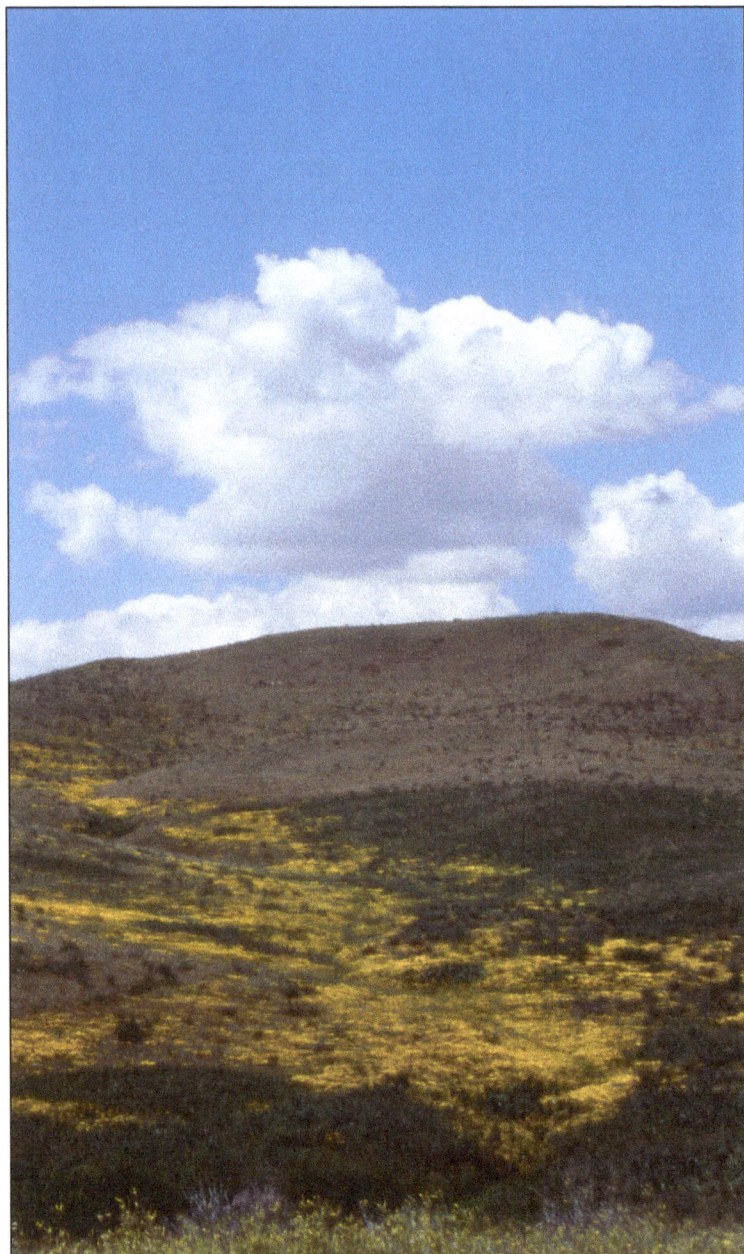

Sweet Clover & Sky

On this Sunday morning in late July, along the back road from Red Lodge, Montana, to Columbus, the rolling hills are green and the sweet clover blooms yellow beside the highway. Some of the alfalfa has been cut, the huge round bales are scattered haphazardly over the fields, drying in the hot sun. When they've traded their green for a pale gold I can't help but think they look like giant shredded wheat, a size perfect for a "breakfast of the gods."

The clouds are starting to pile up above the front range and like icebergs they seem to calve and send smaller parts of themselves off to drift out over the plains. Just like the ice, these puffs of moisture will be worked on by the sun and no doubt dissolve into the elements that surround them before they encounter any sort of Titanic and create disaster. It's always possible, I suppose, that they might bump into some earlier adventurers of their ilk and, like a bunch of unruly teenagers, gang up and try to do some damage to the land below them. Or maybe their new found comrades would be benevolent and together they could bring some rain to an anxious farmer. I know anthropomorfication of animals annoys some people. How about anthropomorphication of clouds? Get over it, I'm a writer and I'll have it any way I like! It's in my job description to look at the familiar in an unconventional way. It doesn't have to be popular, only interesting. What do you think? Will you one day find a moment to muse on the intent of clouds?

The rolling hills along this road look like any other farmland until you notice the clusters of rock and pine that top them here and there. They give away the altitude as I start down from Red Lodge's seven thousand feet to just over half that in Columbus. But the cut hay, some baled, some left to dry in windrows, and the profusion of black eyed Susans, Russian thistles, Queen Anne's lace and green cattails give away the secret that the last days of summer are close.

I've come today to escape the heat. I plan to go to Columbus, catch the Interstate to Livingston and then swing south and enter Yellowstone through Gardiner. I expect a nice cool drive through the Park and then Sunlight Basin and home.

Right now, I'm a little surprised that it's so hot here. I hate air conditioning and though my car can provide it, I prefer (in best dog-like fashion) to feel the wind in my lips, the moving air flowing over my body. Even if that air is hot, it cools me in a way that is far more satisfactory than cold air blowing on me from the dashboard.

I drop down off the foothills onto lower ground. Though it seems late in the season, there is still a bit of cottonwood fluff blowing along the edge of the road where it follows the river. The river itself looks to be only slightly affected by the heat. It is still deep, though in some of the secondary channels the water no longer seems to be moving. I can smell the wildflowers and the newly cut hay. The lushness of the season is evident in the hum of the insects which can be heard even over the air noise from the open window.

It's 2:00 p.m. by the time I reach Columbus and nearly one hundred degrees. I stop at the McDonald's, which seems incongruous, somehow. The idea of some ice cream and a stretch is appealing. The reality becomes the little plastic cup of slushy soft white stuff, over-filled by a careless teenager and, the combination of the poor cup design and sweltering temperature makes it overflow when I remove the lid. It melts faster than I can whittle it down to a manageable level and I must use up some of my precious drinking water to clean the goo from the steering wheel. Ah, the perils of life on the road!

More annoyed than refreshed by that interlude, I take the interstate west toward Livingston and suddenly, one of those clouds moves over the sun and for a few blessed moments I drive in shade. I can feel the sudden drop in temperature, albeit brief. Then the cloud moves on and the sun returns, fortunately not yet low enough to be glaring on the windshield.

The land on either side of this narrow valley is ridged and forested along the tops of the hills. Beehives in stacks of pristine white boxes, nestle at the edges of the fields that border the highway. Pollination with the added benefit of golden sweetness. Take a moment and hold a spoonful of honey up to the sunlight and watch it drip back into the jar. The amber color is as magical and amazing as the deep garnet shade of a good burgundy between you and a candle flame. Miraculous, the beauty of this world we live in.

The Yellowstone River snakes along the base of these hills and nourishes thickets of willows and cottonwoods.

The scattered rocks are lichen covered, spattered with colors that blend perfectly with dry grasses, sage and the pale blond dirt.

Ambling creatures of the night—skunks, raccoons and porcupines—chalk up high casualties along this super highway. It must be quite a barrier to traverse in the dark in order to reach the cool waters of the river. Rare is the animal that can outrun a vehicle traveling at a speed which is only limited by the term "reasonable and prudent."

The patches of over-tall sagebrush indicate that the water table is still high in some of these areas. The cool color of the sage is interspersed with the bright green of the rabbit brush—*Chamisa* we called it in New Mexico—though it is not yet blooming its distinctive sulfur yellow.

I notice that the car's temperature gauge is running a little hot. It seems to drop down to normal and then suddenly back up, dangerously close to those bright red lines. I stop in Big Timber but turns out there's plenty of water. The gas station guy offers the opinion that the heat is affecting the electric switch on my fan and warns me not to take my planned route home which would mean another five to six hours on the road. Unhappily, I turn back to retrace my route, sad to be without the solace and inspiration of Yellowstone today.

Bounty

These trips I make back and forth to Montana afford me some concentrated blocks of time in which to observe familiar territory. I'm grateful for the hours on the road and away from the work that keeps me so busy. While I have a cell phone I rarely use it. I consider it to be something for my convenience and have no need to constantly have it glued to my head. When I travel it's turned off unless I'm expecting an important call or need to make a call myself. I value my solitude and don't understand the need to be constantly connected to others through pointless babble. I'm aided in this behavior by the fact that our cell coverage in this part of the world is spotty, at best.

Today, as summer nears its end, I can feel the signs of the oncoming harvest. It is too soon to see much evidence—nothing is being cut yet but the hay and that has

been ongoing with several cuttings this season. We've had
rain almost daily for the last week, just a quick and heavy
thunderstorm in the afternoon that cools things off. But
rain wreaks havoc with haying, so cutting and baling has
been sporadic.

The death toll on the highway today seems a grim
harvest of its own. Within a single mile is a young 'coon,
a beautiful red fox, a large doe and two skunks. This is the
same stretch where I wrecked my car last year in an effort
to miss a deer.

It had been more than thirty years since I'd collided
with a deer and I had forgotten the cardinal rule: hit it. The
danger is far greater when you lose control trying to avoid
the impact as I was reminded when my car rolled several
times. The deer survived and so did I, but my faithful car
was beyond repair. That the gentle should suffer and die
from our headlong rush from one place to another saddens
me, yet I know from personal experience that the victim
often leaps from nowhere into the path of the oncoming
vehicle with no warning whatsoever to the driver. Do they
sacrifice themselves willingly as a wake up call to those
behind the wheel?

On my last few trips to Billings I have missed the
sight of a flock of sheep who are usually seen in a pasture
beside the highway along with their trusty guard llama. It
takes some getting used to, some effort to identify the
strange long-necked creature who towers above the crowd.
He's the same color as the sheep, and often lying down
when I see him, so it is only that long neck and head that
can be seen over the woolly backs. It has the effect of a Loch
Ness Monster sighting, it makes you do a double take and
think, what was that? Being all too familiar with the
tendency in this part of the world to flat out exterminate
predator species on sight, it gives me hope that there are
some stockmen who are willing to try alternative methods.

I hit the lower elevations and see the fields are still

green with sugar beets and beans. But the haze in the air is evidence of the cool nights and hot days. The river is low, the sandbars deserted. It is too soon for the migratory wayfarers.

As ever, I'm amazed at this strange connection I feel to the land, to the earth. It is understandable, I suppose, for we are of it, we share the same elements with earth and sea. We are of this planet and of this land and it's a shame we, collectively, can't operate our lives on that premise.

I have had a longing to be part of the land since childhood and in a way that goes far beyond gardening. In that department I lean toward more natural landscaping. I have neither the discipline nor inclination toward formal planting. But I do enjoy my vegetable garden, the miracle of walking out and picking something and eating it.

I first made that particular connection about twenty years ago while visiting a friend who owns lemon and avocado ranches in California. All around her house were orange and lemon and avocado trees with fruit far beyond what we see in the markets in this part of the country. We walked out and picked our fruit for breakfast, our avocados for lunch and dinner. The trees at the house were pesticide free and the fruit was gigantic. I remember returning to Wyoming and receiving a box from her a few weeks later. My friends thought her lemons were grapefruit! The avocados were the size of cantaloupe, unrecognizable when compared to the goose egg size specimens at the grocery store which are usually rotten in the center and offered at prices that often skim three dollars.

Her avocados were akin to eating beautiful green butter, and as soft as butter is at room temperature. We ate so many the week I was with her that my silver jewelry turned black from my excessive guacamole burrito consumption. What a wonderful way to indulge! And her dogs indulged, too, laying on the ground below the trees, eating the windfall which made them fat and their coats unbelievably shiny.

In another example of the miracle of food straight from the garden I remember three years ago that a friend gave me a grocery bag half full of fresh peas. I'd only grown snow peas that year and my crop was long over. I shelled those peas of hers immediately, eating many as I popped them out of their perfect green cocoons. Then I steamed them for about two minutes and ate a huge bowl full as my supper. I remember thinking at the time that was what food was meant to be. Nourishment in a way we have quite forgotten as we distance ourselves from the land.

It's funny that tomatoes are the first vegetable that everyone says they most miss the taste of. Almost everyone has memories of what a real tomato tasted like, and is sorry that the hard, flavorless red things that the stores deign to sell us at $3.99 a pound is all we can get today. Yet this is the product that genetic engineers are trying to grow square so that they will pack better. What, exactly, are they thinking?

Well, I grow my own tomatoes so for a month or two each year, I can eat them vine ripe and sun warm. When the frost comes I pick the green ones and ripen them in the house, I freeze them and drink them as juice, make and freeze soup and tomato sauce and put them, chopped, in stews throughout winter. What a miracle!

No, it is not tomatoes I long for but peaches. My memories are of ripe, sweet peaches. The aroma alone sends me into a strange sort of ecstacy. But I always sniff the peaches at the store. Have you noticed they have no smell? Only once a year and sometimes not at all do I find a peach that smells like a peach. When I do, I buy a bag, eat many and freeze some. Even the trucks that show up from time to time from Utah and park by the side of the road to peddle their wares no longer seem to have ripe fruit. And their prices are as high as the store's. Not that I wouldn't pay for the genuine article. It's just that it can so often be a disappointment. Well, my longing for peaches will continue as long as I live in Wyoming. But oh how good they look and how tempted I am when those holiday food catalogues come around. In the dead of winter three dollars per peach almost seems reasonable.

All this only speaks to justify my love of the land and its bounty. It feeds us and clothes us, it shelters us and warms us. It nurtures us and sustains us.

What's not to love?

The Moose Road

I came to Jackson this year anticipating an opportunity to record, on both film and paper, the full splendor of this particular fall. I wanted to immerse myself in this, my favorite season of the year, and do my best to express it in a way that would make it easy for others to understand my feelings.

For three days now I've driven the Moose road, my private piece of heaven, waiting for the sun. But it remains hidden and today the low slung clouds hovering at the base of the Tetons are dripping steadily onto the land below. This, then, is the wet version of this season and I confess it's not bad. Afterall, I love the rain, too.

I have traded my glorious vision of trembling gold for a more static presentation but the trade has been a good one. Every available color of the season is here, spread out on both sides of this narrow road which somehow appears to be illuminated by the *absence* of sunlight.

The moisture has darkened the branches of the bushes, the now-black, spidery lines emphasize the intensity of the shades of red and rust of leaves and berries. All along the glistening dark pavement the yellow foliage seems to glow, accented here and there with a thousand shades of green and sharply defined by the deep rust colored band of dead pine needles that border the black asphalt.

I wonder if it is the hot dry summer that has made so much of this fall. Dried grasses, the warm pale color of old ivory, are a nice mix with the bright yellow of the turning leaves. The willows are so many shades between dull sage and bright yellow—surely an array that doesn't last for long. I wish I could name all these plants. I'm seeing tall grasses going purple rather than gold in celebration, but don't know what they're called.

I get out of the car and walk a bit to study the colors close up and suddenly realize that the flat black shapes scattered everywhere, which I took for stones or small pieces of shale, are thousands of blackened aspen leaves, some broken, others curled up at the edges. In some places the bare trees still sport a few of these dark ornaments, victims of an earlier hard freeze, and I wonder how cold can touch one small patch with its icy finger and leave the five hundred trees nearby to enjoy the season.

These aspens I'd so hoped to photograph in buttery splendor are an unlikely mix this year. Full green stands within yards of full yellow in some groves. Along the foothills green mixes with the gold and patches that have already gone bare. Their naked trunks, in places, top entire ridges like an old man's crew cut—spiky, grey and white.

And the aspens here are an unusual shape. They are tall and slim with balls of branches only at the tops, not unlike Dr. Seuss's Truffula trees. I don't know if they take this height and shape from altitude or because they are so close to the mountain and forced to reach out and up in order to catch the sun.

I pull off the road at the Granite Peak trailhead. Some clouds are still trapped in the branches of the groves that line the steep hills but it has stopped sprinkling for the moment. The parking area is deserted. A huge raven stands sentinel on a fencepost like a great dark eagle. He leans forward when I shut off the engine and untucks his wings for flight, but I talk him out of it. His equally dark double hunkers high in the white bush of a bare tree, watching me.

Following the narrow trail, I marvel at all the colors in the dense brush. Everything is enhanced by the rain. The twisted branches on the ground are blackened, the vivid chartreuse lichen brightened. The wet stones shine as though polished.

The trail forks and I strike out on my own. I high-step over the ground cover to avoid being tripped up by obstacles hidden in its thickness. I think of the careful way deer lift and place their dainty hooves and see that it is habit, the precision of movement required by necessity and expedience.

It is profoundly quiet. There is the occasional scuttle beneath the brush as I walk but I see only a single golden mantled ground squirrel. He's tiny and apparently not a professional beggar for my chirping only warrants a quick double take before he disappears. Even the two ravens have nothing to say. I hear a distant call that could be the honk of a Canada goose but it does not recur and I can't be sure.

This grove is thick and leafless and quiet. White and black, the trunks stand like an army at ease. Not in precise rank and file, but close enough and in great enough number to give one pause.

I am as fascinated by the markings on the trunks today as I was when I first saw aspens in 1962. They look like thousands of staring eyes. These are more stark, more defined than the markings on a birch tree and the bark of the aspen seems to me more aged, more gnarled. What are all these eyes looking at? Or are they looking *for* something? Their lost branches, perhaps?

I decide I'm glad of today's rain. The smell of this wet foliage and damp earth is so different from what it is in summer or even in the wet in early spring.

Shell Falls

When I hit the highway heading east today the air is as hazy and as unattractive as L.A.'s smog. At first I took it for a temperature inversion. The thermometer has been in the forties at night and comes close to a hundred during the day. These extremes tend to whiten the morning air, but this feels more like smoke. Looking out across the basin, the Big Horns are invisible and the lines of ridges and plateaus are only shades of grey against the white sky.

It makes me think about the mystery of light and how it affects my feelings for this land. I can't find anything to love about it in today's colorlessness and that surprises me. I have often said that the land's other half is the sky and that it is the combination of the two that creates the hugeness I love. Without that third element, I am left with a 2-D landscape, and somehow that's just not enough.

It doesn't suit the scope.

Always, the sky is involved in what I see. It is dark thunderclouds and brilliant rainbows, precipitating greys and a hundred different shades of blue. It is a thousand different kinds of clouds in shapes and sizes that you can alter, with practice, by sheer force of will. Even the overcast sky has its subtleties. But today it is dull, flat and uninteresting and I can't imagine how I could love it were it like this every day.

When I moved to New Mexico I was taken with the light. "Mediterranean" they call it, and it is very like the light in the south of France or on the island of Corsica, my only two touchstones in that part of the world. There is a sharpness to that light, a clarity that enhances everything. Van Gogh knew it, was drawn to it, and became obsessed with it as he tried to recreate the miracle of its clarity. It may be what did him in, but, oh, what a way to go! And sometimes I can feel it, too, that nudge toward madness as what you see fills you so full of wonder that you think you may burst if you can't find some way to express it.

In my case, the expression is so much less than the inspiration. I think Vincent felt that way, too. How often artists feel that their efforts fall far short of their concepts and so are disappointed in their work. But perhaps the truth of it is just that a thing is simply what it *is*. You can attempt to capture it in words or images, but the end result is never the original. The creation can evoke feelings of familiarity, of understanding, but it will never *be* the thing it tries so hard to reproduce.

Madness is no threat today. The greyness reminds me of a high coastal fog in southern California that can be expected to burn off by noon and reveal the sky. But here I am, closing in on the Big Horns and they still elude me. Like some David Copperfield illusion, they have now simply disappeared. Foothills, yes. Mountains, no. It renders the view unfamiliar and I realize how much I enjoy being encircled by mountains as I go about my everyday business.

I've seen no antelope on this trip, and I wonder if it is the lack of light. Maybe only certain rays show up their white curves. You can see them plainly in sunlight and under cloudy skies, if you've set your eyes for them. Today, the only wild creature I see is a golden eagle atop a power pole. He looks out at the distant hills. I wonder how he feels about this lack of defined space overhead. I wonder if it makes it harder for him to spot the creatures on which he dines.

Rarely do I have reason or opportunity to go east toward Sheridan and I'm sorry, for the high mountains can be spectacular in the summer months. Today I'm looking forward to the cooler temperatures at nine thousand feet. And today, my meeting is at the top and I won't see the eastern slope, which for me has always been the "green" side.

I start up Shell canyon and pass a cyclist struggling with four full packs on her bike. I can't begin to imagine the dedication it takes to even attempt this climb which is so steep it slows cars to twenty miles an hour as they make their way back and forth up the switchbacks. She's a far better woman than I am.

The air is still thick here. The colors show on the closest rock faces but the peaks are faded. The higher I get, the drier it looks. I'm surprised. The mountain meadows of the Big Horns are one of the lushest places in my memory. There is some rabbitbrush blooming on the way up, but everything else seems sere.

At the top the sky is Wedgwood, more grey than blue, but soft, tentative. At least it's cooler here. I can smell the smoke when I get out of the car and soon learn that twenty thousand acres are ablaze in Montana. We are reaping the aftermath of their tragedy, a cautionary tale delivered courtesy of the wind.

When I start home I still can't get over how dry everything seems. Is it that I have never been here this time of year? Or is this year drier than usual? The meadows that I always think of in terms of jewel colors—deep emerald spattered with the semiprecious tones of the wildflowers— have turned the color of sand. It's not the summer yellow or the gold of fall, but rather the shriveled beige of drought.

Starting back down the switchbacks, I pass the cyclist again, still climbing. In two hours she still hasn't made it to the top.

Disconcerted by the dryness, I stop at Shell Falls. The water is cool, beautiful, peaceful, the canyon mostly shady where the river flows. On the little trails surrounding the visitor center, I can see evidence of fall close up, signs that I missed from a distance. There are a few leaves turning among the green, even on the smaller plants. Some of the aspen have a gold bundle of leaves at the end of a single branch. The rest of the tree still thinks it's summer.

The Return

Heading back to my beloved home range in northern Wyoming, I spend an inordinate amount of time trying to find my way out of Colorado. The path from Boulder to Laporte used to be simple. OK, I admit that was thirty years ago. Today I'm very much surprised that when faced with the thousands of new houses that now fill what used to be section size fields of crops, I cannot find my way at all. My personality is quite flexible and I'm not one to complain that things aren't the way they used to be. (I admit I might be accused of saying things aren't as they *should* be, however.) I seem to take wrong turn after wrong turn. Despite being on Laporte Road at last, Laporte itself seems to have vanished.

So it is with an immediate sense of relief that I leave Cache le Poudre behind and turn onto Highway 287 heading north. Not only am I happy to be so close to Wyoming, but I am, at last, comforted by a landscape that seems familiar.

From the high ground, before I drop down into Virginia Dale, the 360 degree view is awesome. The sky is blue with a few puffy white clouds, and the elevation such that only the tips of the peaks poke above the horizon. The grasses here have, for the most part, gone gold and the bulk of the flower show is over. A few bright black-eyed Susans still bloom beside the road, a few bunches of lavender colored blossoms I don't recognize scatter across the ground beyond the fence.

When I drove to Wyoming for the first time in the late 1960s I remember falling in love with Virginia Dale. I was still in love with a land greener than what I have come to love, but even then I had, for the most part, weaned myself from trees. I'm sad to say that Virginia Dale, like so much in Colorado, has changed in the last thirty years. The little white church, complete with steeple, is still there. And it still looks as though it could only seat twelve people, at the most. But the old Victorian farmhouse with the stately turret is gone, incomprehensibly replaced by a doublewide.

Within three miles of the border you reach the edge of the plateau and look out over what seems must be the whole state of Wyoming. This is my domain of endless horizon and I breathe a sigh of relief. I continue to climb toward the state line. The land is more rocky with scattered pines but at the actual border the trees stop and by the barren landscape, I know I'm back in Wyoming. I wonder if they chose that as the state line for just that reason.

Down the hill, the sweet clover still fills the borrow pit on both sides of the highway. A raven greets me and welcomes me home. I pass Tie Siding, home of the friend of my childhood, Flicka. I'm tempted to see if there might be any place for rent in the area. The idea of being close to Boulder and Denver is appealing, as long as I didn't have to live in Colorado. And I like Laramie, a college town on a more modest scale than Boulder. But with a forbidding altitude of 7277 feet above sea level and a wind that rarely quits, I would probably find the winters impossible. And I must ask the question: could I bear to be so far from Yellowstone?

I have been analyzing over this last week my attraction to college towns. It must be the mix of thought and creativity that arrives with the students and teachers from all over the country. The mood is progressive—despite the horror of Matthew Shepard's murder. It is stimulating in a thousand ways if only because the very air seems to be filled with ideas.

These thoughts lead me to recall my visit to the cosmic bookstore in Boulder. What a treat. Roaming shelves of books on subjects I haven't seen since leaving Santa Fe was entertaining. Barnes and Noble in Billings is the closest bookstore for me and can be very limited. And with books, sometimes you need to fondle them to see if they interest you.

While I was in Colorado I also had a chance to go to Tattered Cover in Denver. They have been a faithful if distant friend since I moved to Wyoming and you have to love them for the owner's stand against the Feds when they demanded she turn over all her records of who had purchased which books. You can call them anytime, talk to someone who is very familiar with their department and order whatever you like.

It's a true old-fashioned bookstore in the very best sense of the word. These are people to whom you can say: "There's this book on anthropology, written by a woman who was studying a group of islanders. I think it was in the south Pacific. It's about six years old and the cover is red. It's about an inch and a half thick." At Tattered Cover they know exactly what you're talking about and will also mention the two books the author has written since. They even know that the tribe being studied was on an island in the Indian Ocean, not the Pacific!

This time, I was looking for a travel book on Greenland—I *must* visit those icebergs! There was no one else in that department at the time and I struck up a conversation with the saleswoman. I asked her if she loved her job. She confessed she did, that she had been a therapist and if a client had talked about working at Tattered Cover as much as she talked about it, she would have told them to get a job there! And so she gave up her practice and has been terrifically happy at work ever since.

If I worked there I would never get a paycheck. They would have to let me hang a hammock between the shelves at night. My passion is books and I could never tire of perusing their stock. Still, the idea tempts me, though I don't think I could return to city life, no matter how wonderful the job.

I have a quick lunch with my friend in Laramie and am on the road again. North of town the land is high and open. The grass is sagey, showing through to the pink dirt. Clusters of fuchsia and purple here and there. The elevated bed of the railroad tracks acts like blinders on the left side of the highway and forces me to concentrate on the landscape to the right. But when the road rises closer to the level of the tracks, I can see the snow fencing where it fans out, a testament to wind and winter.

I am feeling a restlessness as fall approaches. There is so much I want to accomplish this winter and I hesitate to make too many plans because there is a chance I'll be moving. Since I don't want to move, I don't know where to go. I'm just hoping the details of the situation will resolve themselves before the snow flies.

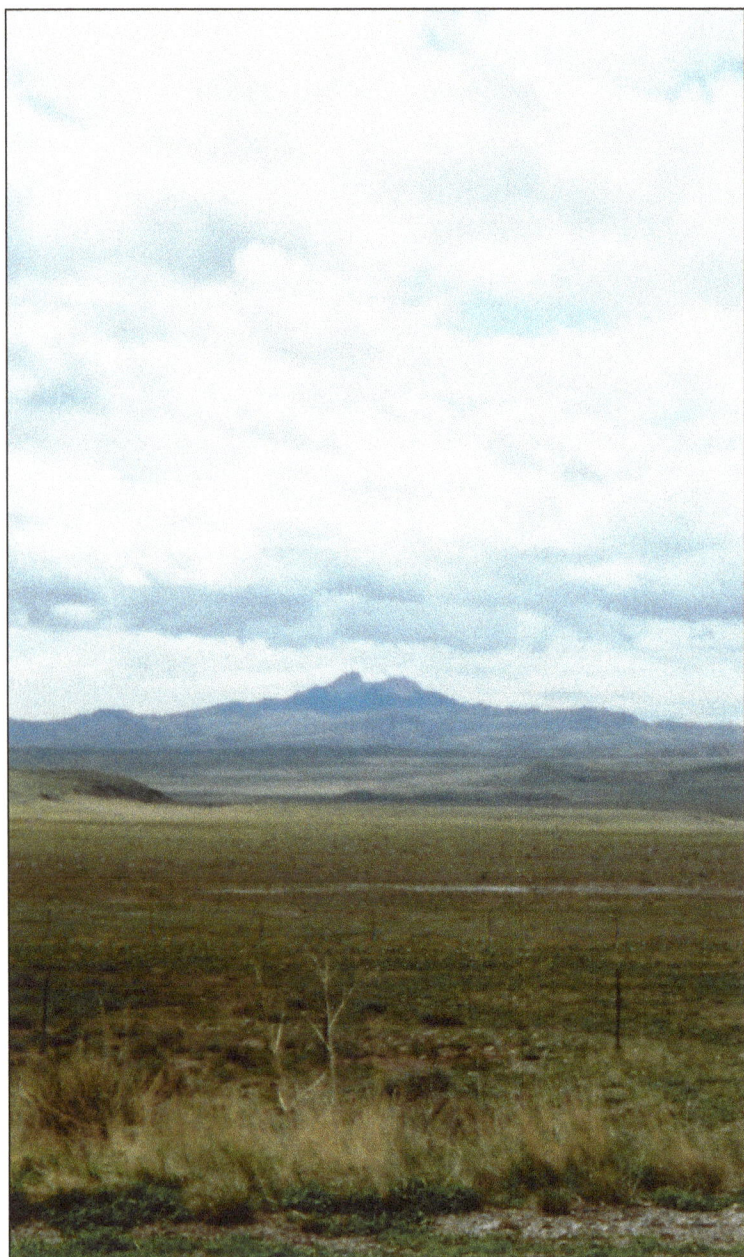

Transformation

On the road again, heading north, I try to observe the change of season that I can feel in my blood but which is still hiding, disguised as late summer. The hills look flat in the morning light against a sky paler than normal. Most of the green this time of year is sagebrush. The grasses have gone to gold in the hundred degree heat of July and early August. Last week's rain brought enough moisture to coax some green along the edge of the road but it is all haloed by straw yellow. Only the alfalfa fields in the valley startle the eye with a shade of emerald that doesn't fit the late summer palette.

Though it is predicted that the mercury will hit eighty-six today, I sense the pending season. After a summer of totally unpredictable weather, I can feel fall coming in the cool air at night. It's my favorite season and

I wish it lasted as long as summer. I mourn it when an early freeze cuts it short and revel in it when it calls itself Indian Summer and lingers even as late as Thanksgiving, though this far north that is rare.

For me the fall is the culmination of what spring and summer have been working toward with such dogged determination. It is the harvest of the bounty of growth, a final labor before winter's rest. Where spring seems to me tender and tentative, fall is bold, solid and self-assured. The vegetation puts on its best in a burst of brilliant color, green currency turning to solid gold as a sacrifice to winter, assurance that there will indeed be another spring.

Perhaps a result of too many tribal past lives, the image of fall for me is always one of the life of summer being laid on the altar of winter as the sacrifice to rebirth. The turning of the seasons is dependable, comforting to me and though the duration and severity of each of them may vary, the cycle does not. Fall is like getting out the featherbed for winter, airing the down comforter and settling in for a snug and deliciously comfortable sleep. And while some people equate fall with death in the same way they do spring with birth, I see it more as doorway, a graduation, a safe and familiar passage into the new year. Of course this is also the way I see death so perhaps there is a correlation here, after all.

I heard a wonderful storyteller at the Buffalo Bill Historical Center many years ago who, in a dimly lit room, whispered to us of bears. It was part of a program on grizzlies but I have to say that while I enjoyed the informative talks by several biologists and rangers from the Park, the storyteller was my favorite. I have been hoping to find the story written down somewhere and so far have not succeeded. But the gist of it was that the bears hibernate because it is their job to dream the spring into existence.

I like to believe it's true. It's a job I would like to have myself.

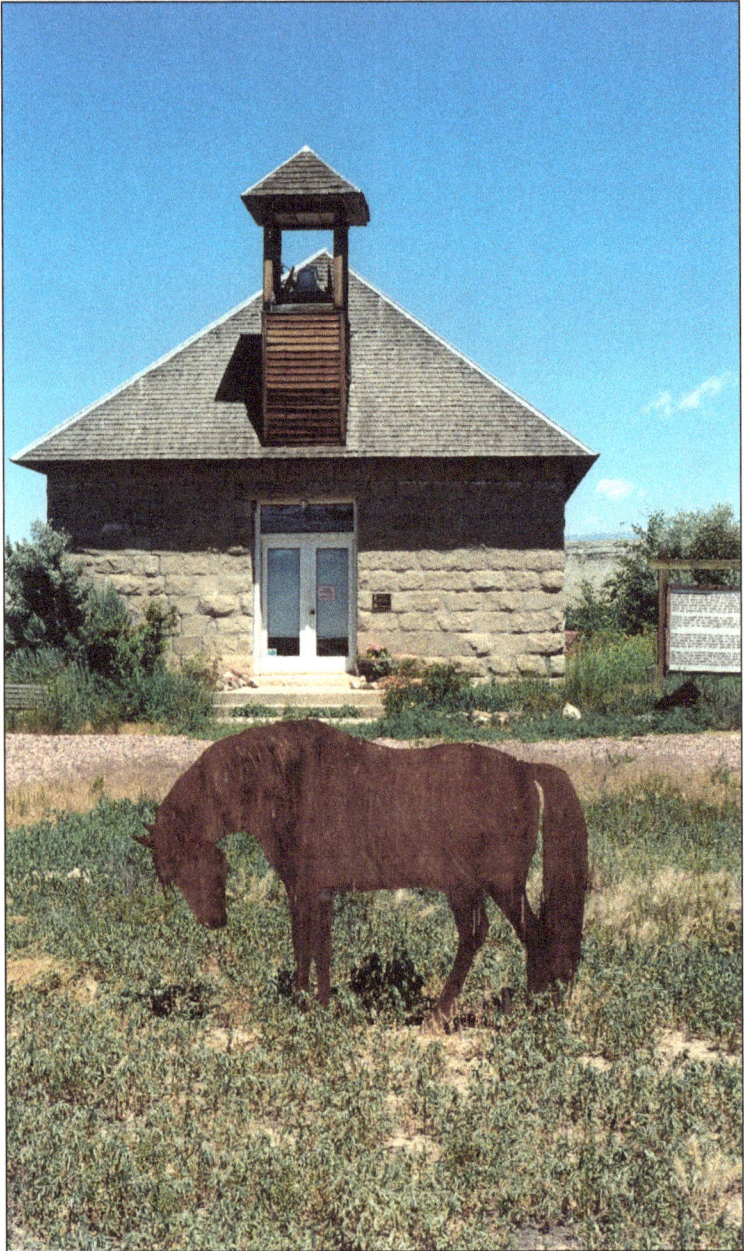

The Stone School

This time as I head east toward the Big Horns I know the haze isn't smoke. At least I haven't heard anything about fires close enough to send their messages to us. The day is sunny, not crisp enough to darken the sky to a true blue but a beautiful October day, nonetheless.

The Basin looks like fall. The cottonwoods are starting to turn and every shade from summer green to gold is fully represented. The clumps of willow along the ditches are bright yellow, outlining the water's path to the fields. The fields themselves are bright green where the alfalfa has been mowed, a darker shade where the sugar beets have yet to be harvested. Other sections, newly plowed, are brown, darkest where the work is fresh and the soil retains its moisture—a fleeting thing in this a part of the world.

I pass twenty or so bales of hay scattered across and along the highway where the field road meets the highway. Someone has turned too quickly and spilled their load. Five miles farther on I find two more bales, blocking my lane completely. As I dodge them I can see they are straw and not hay. I also see they are old, mouldy and understand why no one has stopped to scavenge them.

In Greybull I finally catch up with the overloaded pickup truck that has been strewing its cargo along the pavement. One whole side of the load is gone, the other still piled high. I see nothing at all to indicate the load had been secured and wonder what will be left by the time the truck reaches its destination. On the empty side one last bale hangs precariously, three quarters of the way over the edge, bound to go sooner rather than later. The driver seems oblivious. I'm grateful he continues south while I turn toward the mountains.

I'm considering moving to this area in a effort to get out of town and live a little more rural for a while. I feel a need to hibernate for a couple of years and take some serious blocks of time to work. At least out here, seventy-five miles from distractions, I feel like I might accomplish more. There is also the necessity of cutting my cost of living and this might be the solution.

The place I've come to look at is the Old Stone School that sits just off the highway halfway between Greybull and Shell. I've admired it for years and thought it would be a fun place to live, never realizing that it had been converted some years earlier into a small residence attached to the back of the old school building.

It turns out the place looks like I might be able to squeeze myself and all my possessions into the limited space available. I'm a little concerned about moving this late in the year. Weather is always unpredictable and trying to carry things in ice and snow is dangerous.

On the way back to Cody I try on the idea of living at the school. There was more and better garden space than I'd realized and a good woodstove in the old schoolroom itself which could become a studio for me. The views are spectacular with neighbors out of sight but not so far away that they couldn't be called on in an emergency. I was disappointed by the lack of south facing windows. I always look for solar gain after my wonderful solar house in Santa Fe. That's heat that's even more important in Wyoming's sunny but cold winters. Can I stay warm? Living at the school would mean heating with propane and wood and the predictions for the coming winter are for a cold one.

Still, there is change in the air and it's more than the season. I can feel it.

Silent Morning

Awakening to a deep stillness, I know that the storm is finally over. I look out the window and, sure enough, the white silence outside is the result of the muffling effect of a blanket of snow nearly thirty inches deep. Out another window, I see that I have visitors, the only movement in the sea of white where all but the largest trees have succumbed to the softening effects of so much snow.

The deer paw the snow rhythmically, though it nearly brushes their honey colored bellies. They work in concert, each at a different point under my crabapple tree. Their movements make a precise series: three deep, measured strokes with a front leg—oddly enough it always seems to be the left—four good nudges with an unbelievably shiny black nose, then the reward of a mouthful of last fall's fallen fruit. Heads up, they chew while they watch, ears swiveling like radar to pick up sound and evaluate danger. They swallow and once again stroke the snow, unhurried, methodical.

I study them, fascinated by the perfection of their coats. I know the stiff feel of that coarse hollow hair they wear, but it looks so clean and soft. The color changes as it flows over their bodies, each hair perfect, no hint of disarray. There are no breaks or rends, no tatters to these coats. But the worst of winter is yet to come. Though this snow is deep, the temperature is not frigid. The mercury remains above zero and has not fallen into the range where even the air hurts skin and lungs. Perhaps the deers' perfect raiment will grow shabby if deep snow and falling temperatures make food scarce.

Sharp hooves continue to beat the white to purple-blue as uncertain light changes the excavated unevenness in hue and value. Dogwood and lilac, their spring promise perfectly disguised in sticks of bare beige and burnt sienna, poke through the pristine white at odd angles. No hint now of the concept of landscaping and order.

Still chewing, the deer amble through the as yet undisturbed depths to the huge long needled pines, their quest for sweetness momentarily satisfied. They snuffle among the fallen needles and cones, between the peeling trunks where the snow couldn't find its way to the ground with any sort of regularity. One absently mouths the needles on a low branch. She's not that hungry, rather seems to be tasting so that she might remember if storm and temperature lead to necessity.

The sky overhead is grey and white, the light even. There is no indication of where the sun might be but it's late for the deer. They should have been gone hours ago yet they seem unperturbed. The deep snow has slowed time, confounded the turning of the earth and given us all time to rest.

Winter White

Making the commute between Cody and Billings in the winter months can be a tricky proposition. I'm always grateful when the roads are dry but, being Wyoming, the weather can change very suddenly and a two hour drive in the morning can become a six hour ordeal by late afternoon.

We often get our deepest and wettest snows in March and April. Temperatures fluctuate wildly and two feet of snow can be gone in two days or can plague the streets for weeks. Today I've been lucky and though it is cold, the roads have been dry.

On the way home, as I start the climb to Cody's mile high altitude, the grey sky becomes more threatening. The clouds grow darker, drift lower and become gauzy. They look as though they've been pasted loosely to the dull white sky. Finally, another ten miles down the road, they let loose and begin to scatter a load of pygmy snowballs. These missiles are as far from a snowflake as you can get. They're hard and round and white but tiny. These aren't hailstones. They look for all the world like little beads of styrofoam.

The wind blows them, skitters them off the highway as easily as if it were teflon. They have no hope of sticking. But these winter seed pearls remain where they fall on the on the skewed planes of the fall-plowed fields. The earth is dark, coarse-turned to absorb as much winter moisture as possible. It has succeeded. These dark, uneven furrows, under pressure, turn pure mud.

In single file the silent midnight cattle traverse the unfamiliar pasture like a line of Nubian dancing girls, each dainty foot festooned with an elaborate mudball anklet. The mud has frozen there in dozens of tiny clods that jiggle with each step. This is something new to me. Muddy cows are common, mud jewelry, rare.

The cattle stop occasionally to snuffle one of the few remaining cornstalks. Some still stand straight, others have been forged to odd angles by the plow. They're pale, freeze-dried. A few leaves flutter in the wind like high altitude Tibetan prayer flags, whispering their hopes for the future to the gods of the season.

The light is nearly gone. All is now a stark contrast of black against white; white snow against black earth, black cattle against white hills, white lines against the black highway. Somewhere beneath all this colorlessness Mother Nature is mixing up a stunning palette for spring.

Wind

The wind is unrelenting. It woke me at four in the morning, beating against the little residence attached to the Stone School with such force that I feared the roof might be persuaded to take up the life of a tumbleweed and see the countryside. It moaned and banged, howled and hummed in a thousand unfamiliar voices that twice drove me from a warm bed to investigate the possibility that it had somehow opened a door and was wreaking havoc amongst the as yet unpacked boxes that are stacked and piled everywhere in the old classroom space. But though substantial drafts drifted and eddied around the clutter, the doors held.

This house is new to me though part of it is nearly a century old. In the midst of its windblown distress this should be a comfort, but in reality only the stone walls have endured that long. The roof and the addition have yet to see twenty years. I'm forced to wonder if this will be the night they prove unequal to the task of survival.

The wind did not let up all day and continues to whisper and scream at every seam in the building. By four in the afternoon it still howls and batters this impediment to its will. I look out the window at the adjoining pasture, marveling at the stamina of the invisible assailant.

A clear, tattered, plastic tarp flaps helplessly in the field. It moves inexorably westward like some wounded, crippled ghost grasping at sagebrush as it crawls across the winter-browned ground. There are other spirits out there, some younger, smaller, brighter. They have been left here by the will of the wind and they also struggle for some sort of handhold. They grab on to the power pole as if to catch their breath and then move on. Some slip along the earth as if they hope the wind will pass them by and they can remain in the shelter of the clumps of dried grass to which they cling. But the wind is all-seeing and eventually they are forced to move on.

I watch the snow come toward me, slowly cloaking each row of foothills in pristine white. The peaks still wear their winter mantles but the hills have been dry and brown. Though this wind is nearly strong enough to knock me off my feet, the clouds move at their own pace, a slower one which seems somehow to suit them.

When the wind finally moves on and leaves only a breeze behind, the moonlight reveals that the snow has stopped on the other side of the valley. The hills, white on top, only reflect its brilliant light halfway down their dark slopes. Perhaps tonight I will sleep uninterrupted.

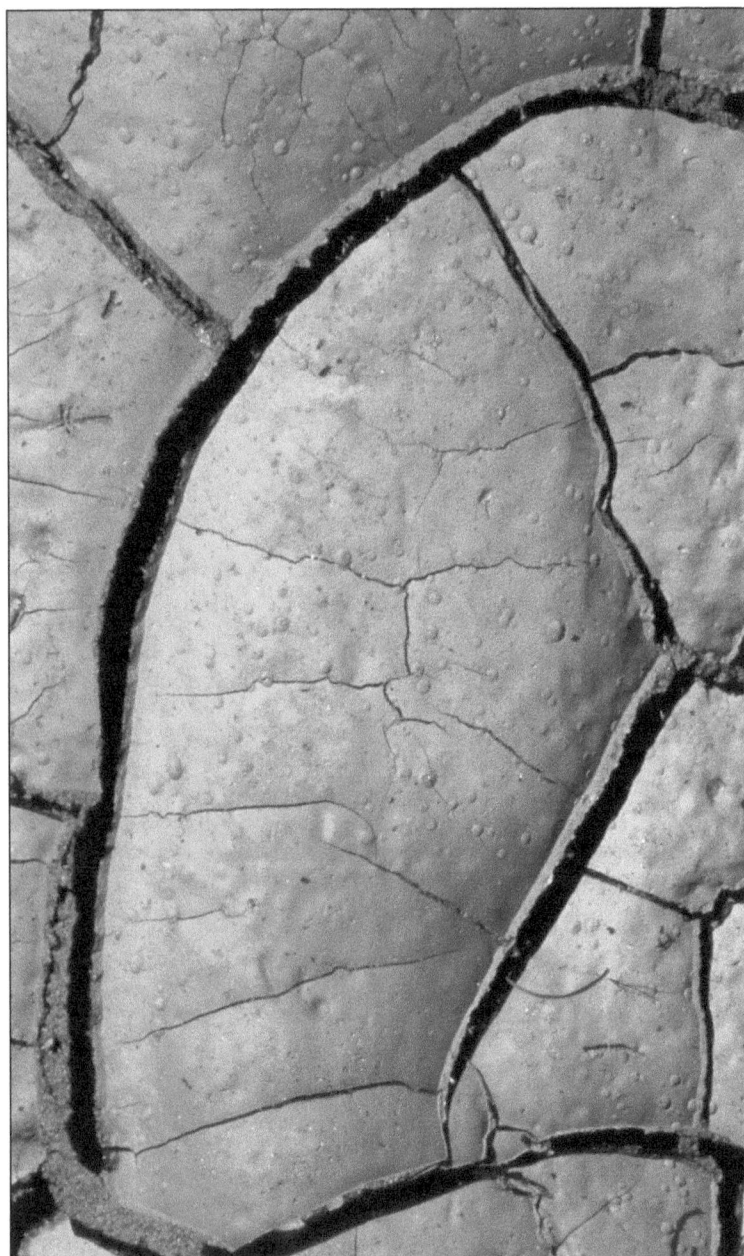

A Closer Look

From the highway, the red of the bluffs against the grey green sage and the gold winter grasses form a foreground for the purple mountains exemplify complimentary colors in both senses of the word. But start off onto that thick golden carpet and you will find it patchy underfoot, tufted with sage and mini cactus that stand only as high as their thorns are long.

The melted snow has scaled the ground, crazing it with a gator-hide pattern of fissures. Those in the east who can't imagine why it takes a hundred acres of this land to feed a single cow, should walk it, see the sparseness of the thin blades that are never green for long, and understand.

Yet there is life here, abundant though for the most

part unseen, which leaves evidence of one kind or another that this is home to many. The rabbits have left droppings in the lee of the sage, footprints in both sand and mud. Horses, too, perhaps wild or only on winter ground, have passed this way. I see signs of the inevitable cattle. Their feet, slipping in the mud as they move down the hill, leave a curious track far deeper at the front as their hooves split and spread to support them.

Standing alone in the center of a bare circle, an ant hill forms a cone, incongruous in its surroundings, a monument of miniature boulders excavated by a thousand busy arms with impossible strength. But where is the army that performed this miracle? Has the strong breeze and doubtful sun granted them a day off? Or have they moved on, bored with this success, seeking another challenge?

Antelope tracks. They have slept in this patch of taller sage. The grasses all around are flattened and must hold the moisture where here they grow thick. It's a case of use facilitating function—flattened grass equals more moisture equals more grass and tall sage to hide behind.

The trails out of this oversize nest lead off in several directions. I walk where they've walked and am soon stepping from one patch of vegetation to another in an effort to avoid the inviting red mud. I smell the crushed sage. Even in winter that plant remembers itself and is still able to give off just a hint of the enchanting fragrance that covers the land after a spring rain.

Two feet away from the mud, the ground is the color of chamois and as dry as talc. I see a lone horsefly, crawling over the uneven terrain, still consumed by seasonal sluggishness, confused perhaps by a fleeting moment of sunlight.

The ground nesting birds are everywhere, their voices sound happy, busy. It is said that in the spring, birds sing leaves onto the trees so they might have a place to build their nests. But there are no trees here. Perhaps the joyful voices of these birds, living close to the earth, can coax from it the first new grass of spring.

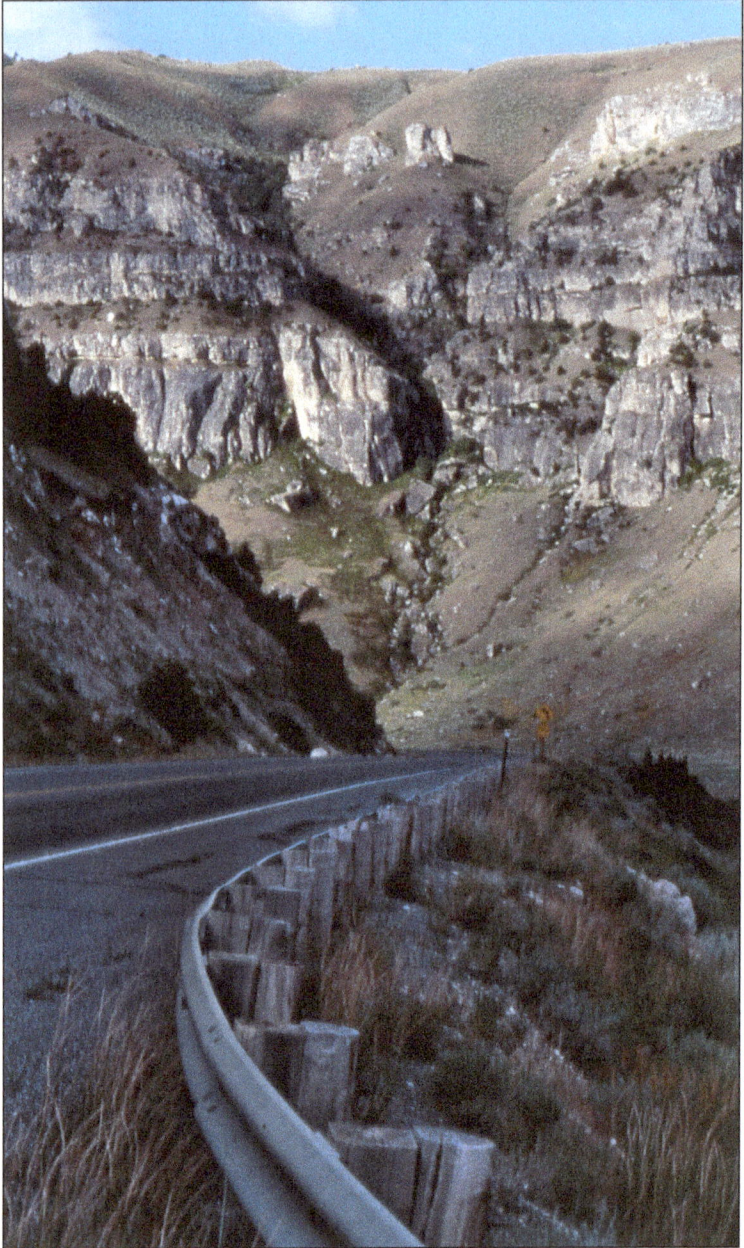

Canyon Walk

From the highway west of Cody, as you drive toward the dam, the walls of the canyon seem proportionate, familiar, manageable. But take a detour on the dam's lower maintenance road, park your car, set out on foot, and you will find yourself in another world.

I walk the road this evening for the first time. The sun is close to setting but here it has long since disappeared behind the rock wall to the west. The river, running a good distance below this road, still catches the fleeting light and shimmers pink and gold to the west while retaining its usual jade green when I turn to look east.

It is quiet. The maintenance trucks have gone for the day, the gates are closed. There is no sound but the water, which is humming contentedly on its way to the plains. The water is low this time of year and the tone not boisterous but rather peaceful.

I start up the road, surprised that it is warmer than I'd expected. Walking along the north wall, I realize I am feeling the residual heat from the day's sunlight which has been stored in the rock and is being released as the air temperature drops.

Every so often, at the edge of the road, I notice a strange type of rock that looks quite out of place among its sharp, angular companions. These rocks are large, I'm guessing in the three hundred to five hundred pound range. But unlike all the others, these are smooth, soft edged, as if water worn. I'm puzzled. They are not gathered together in any sort of group that might indicate they are part of a perpetual seasonal drainage. Some have obviously slid down the steep hillside, but I don't find even two together and none so small that I might pocket them. They are beautiful. I stop to touch them. Like unpolished marble, they're pale with some circular veining in red, reminiscent of tree rings.

I keep looking for some small enough to muscle into my truck so I might take them home and ponder them in the yard this summer. I see none that require less than several strong men and a loader.

Ahead, at eye level, the fading light reveals slabs of red earth which have been exposed when the cuts were made for the road. The red stands out against the pale, yellow stone which is the predominant color of the canyon itself. But as the light diminishes, the colors slowly become diluted and blend into each other.

In this narrow chasm, the still wintering scrub is grey rather than the expected gold of the dry grasses. There are still bits of leaf on the sage and the junipers show near black in the waning light and take on shapes like mysterious dark mountain goats scattered over the steep slope.

I stop to study the vertical wall of the canyon. Steel

power poles march along parallel to the road, yet high above it. Their patina is uniform and brown making them seem to be the wooden trunks of telephone poles. But I'm not fooled. Logic tells me they are many times larger and I can still make out their giveaway hexagonal shape, even in the dim light.

Where the highway crosses the river, the bridge seems inconsequential when you drive over it in your car. At sixty-five miles an hour it takes but a few seconds. It's a brief span, and from below I can see that it is supported by concrete pylons of a precise, clean modern design.

Approaching these amazing pieces of engineering on foot, at first they don't seem particularly large. But when I finally come to stand beneath them, they are huge, rising up to impossible heights like some artist's daring concept for a sci-fi city of tomorrow. Moisture stains them, whether from precipitation or condensation, I can't tell. It drips down the pale concrete of the huge T shaped columns in dark Spanish moss patterns, giving the impression of vegetation where there is none.

The eerie silence beneath the bridge is shattered when a car crosses, its tires whining suddenly and echoing the length of the canyon for a moment before the car and its aural trail disappear.

I leave the bridge behind and continue walking toward the base of the dam, looking up to the top where the rim of stone still catches the light. It is golden now, rich, the color of ripe wheat. The vertical columns of rock are pockmarked with dark spots, caves which make condos with a breathtaking view for the variety of creatures who call this narrow defile home.

When I reach the second bridge, where the road I'm on crosses the river, it is dark and I must turn back. I've only come a mile and I realize this a walk I want to take again, earlier in the day.

The sky is growing darker and the moon is a

bright white, the thinnest of slices of light. I still hear an occasional bird. I imagine they are so excited by the prospect of spring that even the oncoming dark can't stifle their enthusiasm.

If you wish to discover your place in the universe and put your existence in perspective, try exploring bridges. I suggest you start small. Find one that seems to be an inconsequential span over a narrow wash. Stop your car, climb between the fence wires, and make your way to the base of it. You'll be amazed at the size of the smallest of them. What seems perhaps ten or twelve feet high from the road, suddenly becomes forty.

Now, try a bigger one. Move up in size until you feel ready to try something monumental. I guarantee an experience that will challenge your perceptions.

Celebration

I head north, seeking a resurrection of my own this Easter Sunday morning, the spiritual renewal of landscape. Though the sky is cloudy, the subtle hints of the coming spring are visible. The grass along the edge of the pavement is greenest where it receives the benefit of the blacktop; runoff from snow and rain and the residual heat from the road. And there is a hint dark green beneath the yellow green hay that the black cattle are nosing in the pasture. But it is early for this northernmost corner of Wyoming, and as yet, no auras of green halo the bare trees.

The clouds hang low over the ground, pierced by the

hills. The weatherman predicted snow but these clouds carry only rain. I can smell it.

When I hit the shotgun alley of Chapman Bench, the sun breaks through here and there, spotlighting the highway itself and the still-gold grasses on either side.

I cross the river. I can see that the water is low, a dull, pale grey reflecting the sky but a shiny mercury silver in the spots where the sun hits its surface.

Turning off the main highway I immediately come on the harsh boundary lines of burned ditches. They are black-black, too dark to fit in with the subtle colors of the earth. I pass more black cattle, a better black, one that seems more at home in this setting. Within a mile, there are buffalo reclining passively on golden straw that is scattered around their fortified corral. I find something odd about the sight of buffalo confined.

Following the road, I head west toward Clark, admiring the inhospitable, flat and barren land that I love. I almost bought acreage here when I first returned to Wyoming. I dreamed of building a u-shaped house, bearmed into the earth for protection from the relentless wind, and with a vew to the south for miles. Instead I was practical but have always regretted it. Now that parcel has become a subdivision, though I'm happy to see not a single start at destruction has taken place. Yet.

This is land nobody in their right mind would want, which may explain why I love it. It's all cactus, yucca and sage. And, of course, the rocks. They are everywhere and they are big. They are also white and tan, light in color, at odds with any obvious place they might have come from. Some seem to have been here a while. They're covered in beautiful, pale patterns of lichens—gold, orange and sage green against the chalky stone. Others stand at odd angles, some balancing on end like a weird western version of standing stones. But they form no patterns, just seem

to be scattered, everywhere.

Where did these rocks come from? This is no river bottom. The plateau is high above the water. And there are so many of them. The wind blows here with unusual ferocity. It has been known to blow the roofs off of buildings and the pavement from the highway. Have these rocks flown in, carried by the wind, overcome by their own weight as it dissipated, permanently stuck where they landed? Or could they be on the move, inch by inch, foot by foot, a snail's pace migration, noticed only by a vision that could span the millennia? Somehow, I'd like to be here to watch.

My attention strays from the rocks to the houses that dot the valley, more it seems, every time I come. It's a mismatched conglomeration of different styles and shapes. I'd expect to see something solar, bermed into this harsh ground for protection as I'd imagined mine. But this is Wyoming, and the advantages of alternative building styles are hardsell in these parts. I wonder that there are mobile homes. How can they stay put in the gales that rip out of the canyon?

And even more strange to me is the consistent choice to build right on the road. I notice it everywhere I go in rural areas of Wyoming and Montana. It's as though people have found a place to "get away from it all" and yet they must keep a toehold on civilization by having the highway and the passing cars in their front yard.

Finally, I reach my favorite place. From the top of the hill, the thin ribbon of highway falls away into the desolate valley at the mouth of the canyon. Spiky tufts of yucca scatter among the sage and the dried gold grass that shows green at its base. There are a few junipers here as well, hanging on for dear life, flattening out horizontally as if by never daring to grow above twenty inches high, they can creep and spread unnoticed by the wind.

But today the fierce, full-time wind is silent. Perhaps it's calmed by the low slung clouds that cradle the peaks at the narrow entrance to the canyon. There is no sound at all in the valley this morning but the meadowlarks.

I took the meadowlark as a medicine bird years ago, fascinated by their voices. Every time I hear them, I wonder how a lung smaller than my thumb can produce a song so loud and so beautiful. And the ending note makes it sound as though they are asking a question. What is it? I'm grateful that there doesn't seem to be an answer, for they have been asking for a very long time.

I can hear a number of them and I wonder where they are. There are no trees here, no telephone poles. The fence posts are the metal kind and I can't spot a single bird using one for a stage. Yet the brilliant sound is everywhere, no doubt coaxing the spring growth from the ground.

Here, in this valley, is the house that I covet. Actually, it's not the house at all but rather the location. It sits high up on the side of the hill at the north rim and looks out to the south. The view is spectacular. For at least thirty miles there is no sign of human habitation, just curve after curve of land bounded on the west by the front range of the Beartooths. The eye stops only when it smacks up against Heart Mountain which has set itself apart from the foothills. This is my idea of heaven.

The house sits alone, the only one in this part of the valley. I imagine myself living there and with Mickey Mouse as the Sorcerer's Apprentice for an example, I can see myself commandng the winds as they roar out of the canyon. I'm ready. I already have the hat.

My mastery of the elements aside, let's look at things as they are today. The mouth of the canyon is magnificent. There's geology happening here. Lots of it. Varied and in your face. Mammoth slabs of stone seem to be peeling away from the face of the mountain on the south side of the entrance.

I look at it for a long time, searching for some way to describe it. The ridges stand out from each other as though coming loose from the mountain like bark from a tree. Between the ridges, the face above swirls down into a curved canyon, striated, looking like a child's race car track and dropping at an angle as steep as a roller coaster. It's as though the stone has curled up on itself at the open air barrier of the plains and is flaking away at the edges.

Across the road, the rock is completely different. The face here is lighter. Golden slabs stack against the mountain like a sagging row of books, using the range as a bookend. These smooth faces are pockmarked with strange round holes, caves far too vertical for shelter, many of them gigantic. There are big pines up there, too, grabbing a foothold wherever they can. They give some sense of scale to it all, but I suspect that only walking to the base and laying a hand on the stone would bring it home to me. Today, I can only admire the front face where the stones rise up into weird soft edged pinnacles, shrouded in clouds, all leaning like the tower in Pisa, backward into the wind.

Between the canyon entrance and my dream building site is a quickly descending, triple row of brick-orange monoliths. They stand upright like the uncovered remains of some prehistoric lizard. It's not that impressive until you get close enough to realize the scale. Seen from the canyon side, the red extends, curving along the hill face as if some immense clawed creature had taken a swipe at it in anger.

It is time to go and, reluctantly, I turn east. When I pass the buffalo again, they are in the midst of a romp. At first I wonder if something is wrong, but I soon see they are playing. They race out of their substantial corral into their mini open range, tails held high, tongues flopping. Several hop like African antelope, feet together, tossing their heads. It's awkward with their shape, a far cry from a gazell. Their orange plastic ear tags seem out of place.

They come around in a group, pretending to be a great thundering herd of bygone years, and race into the corral again, trying to entice others to join the game.

I pull over to watch. With the new players, they loop the pasture one more time and slow down. Then they stop cold. The jig is up, the game over. A few paw the ground, one goes down to roll. Then they stand motionless, staring south, remembering other lives.

Spring

Today, a week past the middle of May, it finally feels like spring may be firmly established. I take off for Montana on business but anywhere on the road, I can't help but note the seasons as they move over the land.

The rolling hills of the huge Two Dot Ranch along the bench are salted with brilliant dots of pure yellow. Those dandelions which I fight so hard at home are free to express their enthusiasm for the season here. Actually, the war on my home turf is only for the benefit of my neighbors. My lawn is the only one on the entire block that thinks itself wild, the only one dotted with first the yellow blooms and then the fairy puffballs of dandelion seed. Though I sometimes mow daily, the stems are only spun and twisted by the mower blades and within hours are once again standing straight and tall. If it were not so disturbing to those who rue each floating seed, my yard would be wild and I would enjoy the yellow blossoms of the dandelions as much as I enjoy the purple and white of the lilacs.

Here, on the highway, someone has thoughtfully seeded the edges with lupine when the road construction was completed. Today the blossoms sprinkle their brilliant blue-purple along the base of the hills. The green among the blue is new and the dried weeds of last season still tower over the newcomers.

The overcast sky promises the moisture we're all anxious for. It's been a dry winter and continues a dry spring. This year we have the sun we longed for last year. Last year we mourned its absence and complained of the rain. Are we never satisfied with what Mother Nature offers?

Without moisture the sage hasn't taken the barely discernable turn into the season. The color change is subtle in sagebrush but those of us who know and love it can tell when it has decided to start growing again.

As I travel north the clouds look heavy but are holding onto their rain. I smell the air and the glorious scent of wet sagebrush is not on the wind. That would mean that at least it was raining somewhere. I'm disappointed. For me, the smell of sage is the smell of Wyoming. Someday I will live where it surrounds me and even in the dry season I can wet it down in the evening and enjoy it all night!

I lose altitude as I get closer to Billings. Sage hills give way to riverbottom farm land as I drop two thousand feet. There is new growth in the fields here. Some look as smooth and green as a well manicured golf course, the straight lines of the furrows disappearing with a trick of the light. The sandbars in the curve of the river usually sport some of the bigger birds. Today they are empty. But the dried cattails of last year are topped here and there by blackbirds. Redwinged and yellow headed they seem bright jewels against the neutral grasses that are tall enough to hide the new green growth. There is a lushness to the vegetation here that we do not have at home. But I know this landscape. It harbors mosquitos and biting flies for all its lushness.

The poppies here are in full bloom, the lilacs, for the most part, already gone. This drive is a great way to preview the coming spring or to return to linger a little longer over fall when winter has hit home too soon or lasted too long.

Beachcombing

I'm spending this morning as a beachcomber, not at the seashore—they're few and far between in Wyoming—but rather on the shore of the reservoir. There was record high water last year and now the receding level of the lake has left behind an interesting array of freshwater flotsam.

It is the cusp of winter. I begin to wonder if I've chosen the wrong day as the promising sunshine of early morning begins to disappear behind the clouds. Spring hints at its intentions frequently these days but the sensible vegetation here is approaching the coming season cautiously. So am I.

Still, it seems a good morning for a walk and I'm determined to do some exploring.

The clouds continue to move in as the wind flaunts its dominance, kicking up small white caps on the surface of the water and amplifing the relentless lapping of the small waves against the shore. There is no tang of salty air here as I was accustomed to growing up not far from the ocean. Today I smell only cold.

So instead of sandy beaches littered with seaweed, I will wander this sandy coastline strewn with rocks and driftwood.

I begin along the high water line, marked by a sinuous curve of debris that demands that I notice the water was up to *here*! There are a few bone white tree trunks but the bulk of the skeletons are more the size of a broomstick, and shattered into short pieces in their long ride down the river.

It's impossible to resist picking up these ghostly remnants of the forest, their smooth surface is enticing. Perfectly polished by their travels, they are irresistable, silky to the touch of hand or cheek. They no longer have the weight of trees. Somehow, being soaked has lightened them, removed their expected density. And yet, they say that wood left in the water over thousands of years will turn to stone. Must they first become ethereal before they again acquire substance?

I come upon what looks like sawdust, little clumps in the sand. This is puzzling and I try to fit it into some cubbyhole in my brain, find an explanation related to the doings of flora and fauna. But then I see that several larger pieces of driftwood have been cut through. The marks of a saw have left them golden, much more wood-like in color. Someone has taken firewood, or, more likely, hunted out some beautiful twisted roots whose destiny is to become table bases.

I move closer to the water, to the next ridge of debris. This one is of stones. From the highway they appear universally pale and chalky. Close up they seem overcome by the shared tragedy of drowning. They rest in the sand, staring out at the water, unforgiving, without the fluid grace of their river-dwelling kin. These rocks have have resisted the water's influence and maintained their original angular forms.

As I walk, I see that a few have apparently accepted the disaster as an opportunity for transformation. After untold eons in the dry desert air, they have welcomed the inundation and bloomed like roses, split and opened outward in petals of stone. Thus they've returned to the air in a totally new form. These petal parts will scatter over time, granulating into sand. And all this will happen far too slowly for us humans to notice.

I continue to study the rocks in the sand. My eyes grow accustomed to the subtleties and I notice that here and there one rock will assert itself in some bold attempt to be colorful. The most common choice of hue seems to be bright ochre. This is sandstone that can be ground up and mixed with bear fat to make a pigment, a skill I learned many years ago when I was in my "Indian period." The red ones are here, too, brick colored, also crumbly enough to lend themselves to artistic pursuits. I begin to discern more attempts at individuality; serpentine and jade in the greens and some very pale lavender.

Suddenly, there is a scattering—bits of asphalt broken down by the water, black as lumps of coal. These are hundreds of yards from where the water has taken huge sections of the road, and there is no connecting trail between the two. Were these light enough to float? Were the currents along the new shoreline strong enough to move them so far west? Or are they running away from home, embarrassed by their failure?

The wind has won. I start back, cold now. As I walk, I pass some small patches of sagebrush. Their leaves were taken by the flood but I wonder if their roots have survived. Can they grow again? They are very close to the water's edge and when the spring thaw roars down the canyon, they will no doubt disappear again.

I can hear the geese across the water. Their voices are far more bark than honk. The only other sound is the monotonous but soothing slap of the water massaging the shore.

Pronghorn

I adopted the pronghorn antelope as my medicine animal in the early 1970s. I'd not been much aware of these odd creatures until I moved to Wyoming where I had ample opportunity to observe them. It was then that I started into what I call my "Indian period," when I immersed myself in plains Indian history and culture.

In those days, after taking the pronghorn for my personal spirit guide, I hunted him and ate him, tanned his hide with his own brains, carved pipes in his image, made pipe bags from the fur of his throat, decorated his skull with feathers and earth pigment mixed with bear grease, carved boards into the shape of his head and placed a mirror between the horns, painted my tipi with his hoofprints and generally did my best to become one with his spirit.

That was nearly thirty years ago and though my
Indian Period has passed, my fascination with this
unusual animal has not. I see him instantly where others
find him invisible. He still follows me along the highways,
his presence a comfort whenever I travel.

Besides being the fastest animal in North America,
and if I'm not mistaken, second only to the cheetah
in ground speed, the pronghorn antelope is a bundle of
contradictions. His horns are a unique shape, which I
see echoed only in the mouth parts of some of the
larger beetles. These horns seem to grow right out of the
top of his eyes, rather than the top of his head in
the conventional manner of the other horned creatures
that inhabit this country. And his horns are formed from
hair, like a bison's, rather than bone as in deer, elk
and moose. Remove the black horn caps and all you find
underneath is a short triangle of bone at the base. Even
the does and fawns have little black buds, topped with
the same shiny material.

I love the pronghorns for their color patterns which
are more pronounced than those of the other ungulates, and
while more dramatic coloring should make them more
visible, the opposite is true.

The white throat patch when viewed straight on,
looks like wide stacked hearts on some animals, like a
totem of doves with outstretched wings on others. White
bellies and flaring white rumps that signal danger to the
herd are the broader strokes here. The more subtle ones
edge the ears with a fine line of black, another dark "T"
between the horns and down the nose and a precise patch of
black on either cheek.

These creatures even have a little bristly brown
mane. They are so beautiful to me that I have an
overwhelming urge to kiss them on the lips. I know
exactly what that muzzle would feel like though I have yet
to encounter one who would stand still and tolerate

my amorous advances.

These mysterious creatures are perfect in their physical form but seem to have some peculiar habits, like crawling under fences rather then hopping over them easily, as do the deer. What's that about? Their body types are basically the same and yet all the pronghorns' concentration seems to be on running and not jumping.

I like to believe this has something to do with their unwillingness to accept barriers, limitations. These are creatures of the great plains. They never move among the trees, where their incredible eyesight would be useless. While they might shelter in a wash, or amongst the sage, they have all the wide world of the great basins for a home.

And it is a home where they have been relatively unmolested. Many do not like the taste of their meat and so the hunter's bounty often goes to waste. They were never hunted to the brink of extinction like the great buffalo herds, but in the 1930s all of Wyoming's wildlife was decimated by unregulated hunting and an effort was made to transplant the pronghorns back to the ranges where thay had once flourished.

The antelope's distinctive coat pattern renders it nearly invisible against the land. I have driven through the Medicine Bow area where the largest herd in North America makes its home now and, on more than one occasion, have seen hunters stopped by the side of the road, standing beside their trucks in bright orange vests, staring out across the land through their binoculars. I see the small groups of antelope staring back, much closer than where the men are looking.

These animals are also notoriously curious. Plains tribes used to hunt them using "antelope getters," sacred sticks of willow, bent into circles, affixed atop another willow wand, painted, feathered and blessed. The hunters would pick a spot on a ridge, plant the "getters" in the ground, and wait. The antelope would come, unable to resist the lure of feathers that danced in the wind.

I tried this for myself once, long ago. Not to hunt, but merely to call them to me. It didn't take long. Though I saw no antelope when I sat down to wait, in less than half an hour seven antelope approached, coming within sixty feet of where I sat. I chatted them up a bit and then stood to leave. They were wary but held their ground until I had gone.

Rick Bass, in his book *Nine Mile Wolves*, says that some scientists feel the antelope has not evolved, that he has no need of his great speed in the absence of modern day predators. Bass says wolves are what made those legs when, in the days of the great bison herds, they also preyed on antelope.

I'm sure there's truth in his theory but I prefer to think that they run for the sheer joy of it—because they *can*.

9 7 8 1 9 3 2 6 3 6 5 3 6